Thank you for your service to this country and the USD. God bless!

Always in Christ,
Shauna & Anthony
1 Peter 3:15

D0359774

A MILLION THANKS

Shauna Fleming

with

L. A. Stamford

A MILLION THANKS

My Campaign to Send
ONE MILLION
Letters to Our Troops

DOUBLEDAY

New York ★ London ★ Toronto ★ Sydney ★ Auckland

PUBLISHED BY DOUBLEDAY
a division of Random House, Inc.

DOUBLEDAY and the portrayal of an anchor with a dolphin are registered
trademarks of Random House, Inc.

Book design by Judith Stagnitto Abbate/Abbate Design

Library of Congress Cataloging-in-Publication Data
Fleming, Shauna
A million thanks : my campaign to send one million letters to our troops /
Shauna Fleming with L. A. Stamford.— 1st. ed.
p. cm.
1. Fleming, Shauna. 2. Iraq War, 2003—Personal narratives, American.
3. Soldiers—United States. I. Stamford, L. A. II. Title.

DS79.76.F58 2005
956.7044'3373—dc22
2005041251

ISBN 0-385-51570-7
Copyright © 2005 by Shauna Fleming

All Rights Reserved
PRINTED IN THE UNITED STATES OF AMERICA

May 2005
First Edition

1 3 5 7 9 10 8 6 4 2

THIS BOOK IS DEDICATED to all the members of our Armed Forces and their families, past, present, and future. It is through the acts and actions of our military men and women that we enjoy the freedoms we do every day in this wonderful country, the United States of America.

I found these words etched on one of the memorials inside the Pentagon for those who died on September 11, 2001:

"It is the soldier, not the reporter
who has given us freedom of the press.
It is the soldier, not the poet
who has given us freedom of speech.
It is the soldier, not the campus organizer
who has given us freedom to demonstrate.
It is the soldier, not the lawyer
who has given us the right to a fair trial.
It is the soldier who salutes the flag,
whose coffin is draped by the flag,
who allows the protester to burn the flag."

— CHARLES M. PROVINCE

CONTENTS

ACKNOWLEDGMENTS

I BELIEVE I HAVE BEEN LED down the road to "A Million Thanks" for a reason. I would like to give thanks first and foremost to my God and Savior, Jesus Christ, who has opened doors and motivated the hearts of Americans to "move mountains." Without my faith in Him, and His plan for me, I would not have accomplished this mission.

I also want to thank my mom and dad for their support, especially for my dad's "coaching" sessions.

To my Grandpa Nate, who probably has helped spread the word of "A Million Thanks" more than the media ever could, and my Grandma Betty for all her work on my five "memory books" and for her organization skills, which still have not rubbed off on my family, thank you so much.

Thanks to my Grandma Lorraine and Grandpa Richard,

who, even while living far away from me, keep supporting and encouraging me, always calling for updates.

Thanks to my Aunt Sandee and Uncle Mike for staying up late with me organizing and sorting mail, and for their constant support.

I appreciate, too, the support and financial help from my Uncle Dave and Aunt Nancy, and their businesses Skateland and Mountasia Fun Center.

A big thank-you goes to my two great friends Allison See and Kelcie Pinick. Without them, this campaign would not have been the success it has become. They have stuck by me and helped me with whatever was thrown my way. Not to mention keeping my head on straight when I was stressed.

I also want to acknowledge other friends who have become a memorable part of "A Million Thanks": Matt Hall, for lending his incredible voice, lasting friendship, and help when I needed him most; Adam DeCarlo, for his support and friendship when all this began, not to mention a common love for a certain show; Matt Barnes, for his "I'll drop whatever I'm doing to help you" attitude and support even when we were BFE; John Andersen, for being a great friend and a NASCAR fan when the others aren't; Steve Nelson, for being at almost every "A Million Thanks" event and keeping us all laughing; Katie Canseco, for being Katie Canseco, who always smiles and wants to be on TV; and SuZanne Kelley, for her support and willingness to help me with anything that I need at a moment's notice.

★ X ★

A big thank-you goes to the rest of my friends and classmates at Orange Lutheran High School for their support, and for believing in me at the very beginning. Also to my principal, Mr. Gregg Pinick, for taking a chance on me and being open to my idea when none of us knew how big this campaign might become.

I want to thank my teachers, this year and last, who have been so incredibly patient and accommodating when I had to miss class. My special thanks to Mr. "Coach" Tom Howard, who is also my basketball coach, and to Mrs. Vicki Schulte. The two of them stepped up to be the overseers of "A Million Thanks." Also, thanks to my JV basketball coach, Coach Mark Lofink, for being understanding when I had to miss practice but still giving me the chance to play in the games.

Pastor Tom Rothhaar and his wife, Laura, and the members of Light of the Canyon UMC Church, where my family worships, have participated in all of our military support campaigns. What a wonderful church family I have.

I want to thank those members of the media who took a small story and helped me spread the word, enabling me to attain my goal. Eric Carpenter of the *Orange County Register* started the ball rolling with a wonderful kickoff article. Our biggest break came from an Associated Press story done by journalist Gary Risling. That story put "A Million Thanks" all over the country. Thank you, Gary.

A big thanks to Linda Vester and Michelle May of Fox News. They were first to put us in the national television spotlight. Thanks also to Barbara Chen and David Muir and the rest of the gang at ABC's *World News Now* for their push too.

I guess I could say the woman who really gave me the incentive to start "A Million Thanks" was Alice Wax. Alice is the founder of National Military Appreciation Month. She taught me the meaning of persistence and never giving up. She is a true American in every sense and I thank her so much.

Chris Murch, president of wsRadio.com, and his staff gave me the chance to tell the world about my campaign on my own wsRadio.com radio show. I thank him, Lee Mirabal, and Wade Taylor.

I met Robert Weinberg on an airplane. He thanked me for what I was doing, and now I must thank him for being my wonderful lawyer throughout this journey.

Thanks, of course, to our sponsors, who are listed at the bottom of my Web site, www.amillionthanks.org. All of these people and companies either donated cash or services to assist with the postage and pizza costs for sorting parties.

My Webmaster, Mike Mitchell, gave me the first design for the "A Million Thanks" site. Glen Christiansen took it to another level. Neither charged me for any of their work. Thank you.

To Doug Mahr, who opened the door and submitted my story to Peter Miller and his staff at PMA Literary Agency, and also to Peter, who took a chance with me, I appreciate you both very much. To Michelle Rapkin, and everyone at Doubleday, for guiding me along. And, of course, to my wonderful coauthor, L. A. Stamford, for taking so much extra time to work with me, a million thanks and more.

The greatest supporters of "A Million Thanks," however, have been the passionate Americans around the country who don't mind taking two minutes to write a quick thank-you to the people who need it the most: our soldiers. I want to thank everyone who has ever written a note of thanks, said thank-you, or even said a prayer for our troops. They sure need it.

My last thanks go to our military for their endless support and love for this great country. They are the ones who have made "A Million Thanks" possible, and without them our country would not remain as free as it is today. Though I have had much contact with soldiers near and far, I want to thank my two heroes, RP3 Everett Headley and Private First Class Michael Byrd, who were the first to contact me from Iraq using cell phones and e-mail. They taught me what it is really like to be a soldier in Iraq, and what it is like to put your life on the line every day. A big thank-you goes to Sergeant John Metzler, who has become my great friend, and who helped me through some of the toughest decisions I had to make during "A Million Thanks." For his strength, love, and passion I am forever indebted.

To all of you who have helped, and to you the reader, I say, "A Million Thanks!"

CHAPTER ONE

The Beginning of a Remarkable Journey

A S WE RODE ON THE TRAIN from Anaheim to San Diego, I had no idea that my life was about to change. The Amtrak Surfliner was great, and I loved looking out the window to see all the sights. Against the deep blue Pacific Ocean, I saw people surfing near the San Onofre power plant because the water is warmer closer to the reactor. There was a line of cars waiting to get through the border patrol's checkpoint, and U.S. and Marine Corps flags flew high over Camp Pendleton. I saw the tall buildings of San Diego State University where I would later dorm during a basketball tournament (we placed fourth out of sixty-four teams that weekend). The marine training facility near the beach buzzed with activity, with helicopters hovering, tanks in motion, and navy ships anchored just off shore.

All of this was fascinating to look at, but it didn't diminish the fact that I really didn't want to be there. It was Thanksgiving Day, 2002, and we were supposed to be home having dinner together as a family. Instead, my dad agreed to arrange a meal for a few hundred strangers—soldiers and their families—at the USO. I knew he had been involved in doing things for the troops, collecting valentines Americans wrote for them and that sort of thing, but at thirteen, I didn't really pay much attention to any of it. All I knew now was that this wasn't going to be a *real* Thanksgiving. Yes, our family was going to be together (my younger brother Ryan, my mom and dad, my Grandpa Nate and Grandma Betty, my Aunt Sandee and Uncle Mike, and me), but we would be eating with hundreds of people we didn't know.

When we got to the USO, though, I started to feel differently about things almost immediately. The people there were either soldiers back on leave or family members of soldiers who were away defending our country. Most of them lived on bases, and this USO was the closest thing they had to home. They didn't have much of a choice about where they were going to spend their Thanksgiving. I could see they really appreciated having a place to celebrate and that people cared enough to do something like this for them. It made me feel a little guilty for complaining to my parents earlier about having to make the trip.

We began decorating the upstairs hall for the Thanksgiving meal. There were rows and rows of tables. My mom and aunt hung *Happy Thanksgiving* signs and pictures of turkeys and pilgrims. My dad, my brother, and I set up an area with games in which soldiers and families could win prizes my dad had delivered there earlier that week. The rest of our family helped the cooks finish preparing the dozens of turkeys in the USO's huge kitchen.

A few days earlier, the USO had called my dad for help when their main food donor backed out at the last minute, leaving them with no food to serve. He'd helped them out in the past with donations of prizes for various events, and they knew he was in the fun center and restaurant business. My dad enlisted the help of Kevin Davis, the CEO of Bristol Farms (a large grocery store chain) and the father of my friend Kristen. He agreed to donate most of the food.

While we served dinner, I looked around the room and thought it was great that Kevin and my dad had helped the USO and these people so much. Amazingly, it seemed like a traditional Thanksgiving (if your family was really, really huge).

After the meal, I operated a spinning wheel where kids could win prizes. This was a big deal to these kids because money was tight for most of their families, and the kids couldn't simply get toys whenever they wanted them. There was also something called the Santa Store, which the USO runs before Christmas for military families who can't afford gifts for each other. At the Santa Store, stocked with donations from local businesses, they can pick gifts for each other without charge. Throughout the USO, there was a real sense of festivity, and I could see it was a special event for everyone involved.

Seeing the looks on people's faces as they ate, played games, and chose Christmas presents, I began to realize how important something like this was to them. They weren't with their extended families, as they might be on holidays when they or their loved ones weren't in the service, but they were with people who understood and appreciated what they were going through. Suddenly it didn't seem like such a big deal for me to give up my normal Thanksgiving. In fact, this kind of Thanksgiving started to feel pretty good.

The most touching moment—and the one that literally changed my attitude toward the military—came when my dad handed out some of the valentines he'd received late during the previous February. He walked over to a soldier about to leave and gave him a packet of valentines. The soldier seemed amazed at the gesture.

"There are a lot of people who appreciate what you're doing for them," my dad said.

I could tell this really touched the soldier but also that he wasn't accustomed to this kind of treatment. He looked my dad in the eye and said, "Thank you, sir." Then he turned to go. As he walked away, though, I saw him wipe away tears. I looked back at my dad and saw he was doing the same thing. That's when everything clicked for me. At that very moment I realized how much our appreciation meant to our troops, and I really wanted to let them know how much they meant to us. As we rode back on the train that night, I had a completely different feeling in my heart than I'd had on the ride down.

A few months later, just before Valentine's Day, we went down to March Air Force Base in Riverside, California. (March AFB has a history that goes back many decades. Bob Hope performed his first USO radio broadcast from one of its hangars.) Security was extremely heavy because things were heating up in the Middle East. When we pulled up, some soldiers directed us to a special "holding area" for large vehicles. Several soldiers then inspected every inch of our van. When one of them opened the back and asked what was in the boxes there, I said, "Valentines…Would you like some?" He smiled and said "Maybe later" as he looked through them to make sure they were, in fact, valentines.

They escorted us to a meeting room in a hangar where the soldiers who are being deployed wait for their flights. The room was full of uniformed soldiers, all of whom were pilots. The war in Iraq was about to begin and the pilots here knew that in the near future they would find themselves in harm's way on a daily basis. My dad and I gave them boxes and boxes of valentines. The pilots were stunned that so many people had taken the time to make them. They were even more amazed to discover that the valentines we delivered were a small fraction of the number we collected.

I held up a couple of huge banners made by some elementary school children. One in particular attracted a lot of attention. It consisted of red, white, and blue handprints that formed the shape of an American flag. One of the pilots asked for it; he said he was leaving the next day for the Middle East and wanted it for his tent. As I looked around I could see intense emotion in the eyes of these military people. Many put the cards we handed out in their duffel bags, and I knew those valentines would be going halfway around the world very soon.

I can only imagine how nervous most of the soldiers in the room were that day, not knowing when they would be shipping out or what was going to happen to them in the near future. The looks of appreciation on their faces, however, went straight to my heart. We had done something so little compared to what they were doing and what they were about to do, but it meant so much to them. This reinforced for me how important it was to be involved in projects like my dad's, to do everything I could to help them feel as good as possible about what they were doing. If our troops were going to war to defend us, I wanted to make sure they knew just how much we appreciated their sacrifice.

★ ★ ★

THAT FALL, I started going to Lutheran High School in Orange, California, and it was a busy time for everyone in my family. I was in some tough classes and adjusting to being in a new school with mostly new people. I was also on the basketball team, and practices took a lot of my time—so much that I had to give up my Tae Kwon Do lessons. It seemed that all of my days were full. At least, that's what I thought.

Valentines for the troops were still being sent to our church because so many people heard about what my dad had already done, but he wasn't able to run an all-out campaign the way he had the year before. In March, I realized that the activity had become really important to me. I missed it, and felt that I was letting a lot of people down by not doing more.

One night, I went up to my dad's office while he was working away on his computer. I told him I felt bad that we had let Valentine's Day go by without doing much for the troops. Considering that a war was going on, I felt embarrassed that we were too busy with our own lives to show appreciation for people who were doing so much for us. I told him I wanted to do something to show the troops that we really cared for them.

I knew that I wanted to do something, but I still didn't know what it was. Finally I decided that I would collect thank-you letters from all over the country for our troops. This would show them that all of us at home were thankful for what they were doing. I went back to my dad and told him. The year before, I had joined him on a trip to Washington, D.C., where he'd helped his friend Alice Wax gain support in her drive to establish an official National Military Appreciation Month (NMAM) every May. I told my dad that I wanted to collect the thank-you letters as my contribution toward NMAM. He told me he thought this was great, but said I should have a specific goal in mind.

"Why don't you try to collect a million letters?"

He probably thought this was going to intimidate me in some way, but that number didn't sound scary at all. I just looked at him and said, "Okay, I'll do it."

Now I needed to come up with a name for my project. I again went to my dad, who is good at that kind of stuff. He said that my "project" was actually becoming a "campaign," and he suggested calling it "Thanks a Million, Troops." Since I knew we needed a Web site to extend our reach, I searched the Internet to see if I could get a Web address with "Thanks a Million" in it. Unfortunately, all of the "Thanks a Million" URLs were taken. We thought about it some more and decided to try "A Million Thanks." The Web address www.amillionthanks.org was available and we quickly snapped it up. The "campaign" now had a name.

I knew I would need a lot of help to make this happen. Since my school requires every student to work on community service projects, I thought it would be a good place to drum up support. To get my school's backing I would have to start at the top, so I went to see my principal, Mr. Gregg Pinick. It was a little strange for a freshman to ask for an appointment with the principal and I felt a little awkward about it, but I kept telling myself this was really important.

When I told him my plan, I expected him to ask me a lot of questions and to be skeptical about my ability to do anything on that scale. Instead, he was immediately positive. He told me he thought it would be a great service project for the students, but if I was going to pull something like this off, I had to present the idea to the faculty. I needed the complete support of the teachers in order to get a large number of students involved.

As a freshman, I really only knew my own teachers, and as my mom drove me to a faculty meeting that Friday, I had no idea what to expect. Would the faculty stand up and applaud? Would they think this was a stupid freshman idea? Would they just ignore me? What if I made a fool of myself and for the rest of my high-school career teachers came up to me saying, "You were that really weird girl who tried to speak to us about your dumb idea"? On top of this, Mr. Pinick, who I knew was on my side, wasn't going to be at this meeting; Mr. Kevin Kromminga, the vice principal, would be introducing me instead.

My mom drove me to school and said she'd wait in the car. Before I stepped out, she said a prayer for me, which helped calm me down a little. The faculty meeting was on a day when there were no classes, and I'm sure some of the teachers wondered what I was doing there. It was a little awkward, but I just had to tough it out.

Finally, the vice principal called me up. I went to the front of the room with a poster board on which I put pictures from our Thanksgiving with the USO and our visit to March Air Force Base. I also carried two handouts; one was a timeline of what I planned to do and the other was a press release that my dad had prepared to announce the kickoff of the program.

It was only then that I realized I'd never done anything like this before. I once heard that a poll found that more people would rather be the one in the coffin than the person speaking at a funeral. I wasn't afraid of public speaking, but this audience was different from any I'd ever addressed before. I started talking and looked around the room to see how people were responding. The teachers who had me for a student seemed to be paying attention, but the rest of the teachers seemed only to be listening casually. This wasn't good. If I only had my seven teachers against the other hundred, my plans weren't going to get very far at all.

Toward the end of my presentation, I remember feeling strange. I'd fainted before when I got really sick, and I was getting that feeling now—things were going black and I was only seeing the outlines of people. I couldn't even hear myself speak. I thought, *Oh no, this is going to be so bad if I pass out in front of all these people.* I didn't actually feel nervous, but I think this feeling of blacking out was the result of my nerves catching up to me. I don't think I realized until that moment just how important it was to me for this to go well, and how worried I was that I might not be able to spark their interest. Then, on top of feeling like I was going to faint, I started shaking. I was sure I looked totally ridiculous in front of these people, most of whom had never seen me before. Knowing that I needed to finish up before something completely humiliating happened, I quickly thanked everyone, told them there were pictures to look at, and went to sit down.

When I sat, I didn't feel as shaky anymore. That's when I noticed that everyone was clapping. Mr. Kromminga went to the front of the room, told all of the teachers that he thought "A Million Thanks" was a great idea, and urged them all to support it. Amazingly, in spite of what I was feeling, things had actually gone well. I didn't throw up. I didn't pass out. And people seemed to like what I had to say.

Now that I had the principal, the vice principal, and the teachers on my side, I needed to get the students involved. I went to Pastor Detviler, the campus chaplain, who is in charge of all the chapel services in my school. I asked if I could present my program to the entire student body at morning chapel, the point each morning when the entire school (students, teachers, office staff, etc.) assembles in the gym for a time of devotion and updates on activities. He agreed to let me make my presentation to the students on the following Wednesday.

The next several days were extremely hectic. I began working on signs with my mom and friends. A local company donated a banner, and my dad wrote another press release about the campaign and the kickoff at my school. As the day approached, I felt I needed to have some soldiers with me who could tell the students how important mail is to them. A family friend, Joe Koontz, is a former marine, and we asked if he could help us. Within a few hours, Joe had three soldiers lined up for me: Corporal Frank Guerra, Sergeant Carlos Aguilera, and Staff Sergeant Gary Bolfa. Two of them had just returned from duty in Iraq, and all agreed to attend the assembly in uniform.

The day of the assembly, we decorated the gym with red, white, and blue balloons and posters. Right before it started, Kelly Reid, a student in my English class, came up to me with a packet of letters and said, "These are for you. They're from the kids in my mom's Sunday school class."

My dad saw this and said, "These are the first letters of your million. You need to present them to the soldiers here today."

The students began to enter the gym, and once again I felt really nervous and started shaking. Several of my teachers and a bunch of my friends came over to me, gave me hugs, and offered encouragement, telling me they knew I was going to do great. This was a huge help. Still, when I looked out on the 1,100 students assembled there waiting for me to speak, I felt a little overwhelmed. This was by far the biggest group I'd ever spoken in front of, and what I had to say to them was tremendously important to me. I couldn't allow myself to mess up. Just before we started, I noticed some people from the media come into the gym carrying television cameras. I thought, *Oh great, now I also have to speak in front of television cameras.* This made me even more nervous because I had never spoken on television before.

Mr. Pinick introduced me, and as I walked up to the podium to speak, the one thing that went through my mind was *Don't trip.* There were all kinds of cables on the gym floor, and I was sure I was going to fall over one of them and make a fool of myself. I guess this is the kind of thing you think about when you don't want to think about what really concerns you. I made it to the podium without falling, though I was still nervous. But when I started to speak into the microphone, saying, "Thank you all for coming," I calmed down instantly.

"We have an opportunity to make a difference in the lives of military men and women by thanking them for putting themselves on the line and sacrificing for us every day. 1 Thessalonians 5:11 says, 'Therefore, encourage one another and build each other up, just as in fact you are doing.' This is our theme verse for this project. We're going to collect a million thank-you letters and e-mails of appreciation for National Military Appreciation Month. The letters will come to our school from all over the United States, and we will deliver them all over the world."

I gave the students details about the project and explained how they could get involved. Then I introduced the soldiers who had come to join us.

Corporal Guerra spoke first. As he walked up to the microphone, I handed him some of the letters Kelly had given me and told him these were the first ones from my campaign. He smiled as he took them. He was wearing his combat fatigues and seemed a little nervous. After introducing himself, Corporal Guerra said, "Mail is one of the most important things a soldier can get. I found out that my wife was pregnant through a letter I received from her." At that point, the gymnasium broke into thunderous applause. "I encourage all of you students to get involved and to send a letter to our soldiers." He wound up speaking only a minute, but his message came through loud and clear to all of us.

Staff Sergeant Bolfa was dressed in his sharp marine "dress blues." I gave him his letters and he stepped up to the microphone. "Good morning, Lutheran High School. My name is Staff Sergeant Bolfa. I am your local recruiter, and have been for the past few years. I want you to know that mail takes the place of phone calls when phones are not available in Iraq. I can't emphasize enough the importance of mail. These guys have been there and know that."

Sergeant Aguilera came up next and was most appreciative of the letters I gave him. He also wore his marine dress uniform. He had seen quite a lot of combat while in Iraq. There had even been a book published telling stories about him and his unit. "I got a lot of mail from my family and friends but the real important mail came from people I didn't know. When I would get those kinds of letters, it reminded me of the reason I was over there. When I got back, I made it a point to meet or contact everyone who had sent me mail while I was over there fighting." When he finished, there was a roar of applause.

I returned to the microphone to end with a prayer. "Lord God, I thank You for this opportunity to brighten so many people's lives. Please guide this and send it in the direction You want it to go. Place it in every one of these students' hearts to be involved as much as possible. Thank You for the protectors of this country and keep them safe and in Your arms. In Jesus' name I pray, Amen."

Matt Hall, a senior and one of the top drama students in my school, sang a beautiful rendition of the National Anthem—the perfect touch to end with—and then we were finished.

I was so awed that everything had gone as planned. It felt like it had all happened so quickly. While the students filed out, two TV stations and someone from the *Orange County Register* came by to interview me right on the spot. Afterward, my friends gathered around and congratulated me. It was an incredible feeling, having gotten a project that was so important to me off the ground, and knowing that I was going to have plenty of support in doing it.

The *Orange County Register* ran a story about the assembly and "A Million Thanks" the next day, along with three pictures. This, combined with the other interviews I had given on the day of the assembly, kicked off a level of media attention I never would have dreamed possible. I expected people to respond positively to the campaign, but I had no idea they would respond *this* positively.

A couple of days later, I had a softball game that I was really excited about because my coach had told me I would be starting at first base. Until then, I'd spent all my time in the outfield. But this was going to be a memorable experience for more than one reason—news radio station KFWB was sending a reporter to do an interview with me during the game. While it seemed a little strange to me to do an interview in this setting, I felt very comfortable answering the questions from the friendly reporter. It was an odd feeling, though, to be sitting in the dugout with my friends one minute and then doing a radio interview the next. That's the kind of thing you see in the major leagues, not at a girls' high school softball game. (As it turned out, the interview went well, but the game didn't. Mater Dei, a huge rival, smashed us.)

We sent a copy of the kickoff press release to the Associated Press newswire service. The next day an AP writer called and left a message on my dad's home business line, which had become the "A Million Thanks Hotline." I called the writer back, not really knowing what AP was in the world of media companies. When I told my dad at the dinner table that I had done an interview with the Associated Press, he excitedly said, "Oh my gosh, AP called you?" He then got *me* excited by explaining that AP was one of the best ways to get the word out to the world about "A Million Thanks." If I had known they were that big, I probably would have been a lot more nervous talking to the writer, so it was probably a good thing I didn't know.

A couple of days went by and then all of a sudden the "hotline" began ringing off the hook. Hundreds of newspapers from all over the country picked up the story. As a result, radio and television stations from these places requested interviews with me. The story of "A Million Thanks" was quickly in the media everywhere.

I was getting ready for school one morning when the phone rang. It was Fox Network News producer Michelle May, telling me that Fox wanted me to appear on the cable news channel's live national television show *DaySide with Linda Vester* the next day, and that they would send a car to my school to bring me to a studio in nearby Anaheim in the morning. This stunned me. Fox News was not only a nationwide news network, but a worldwide one as well. Michelle said that many of the troops over in Iraq watched Fox News via satellite, so my message would reach them, too. I knew this could be a huge help to the campaign, so I agreed immediately.

Michelle said Fox wanted my dad on the show with me. I thought this would be good, as my dad could do the talking—I was a little nervous about *live national television.* When I told him, though, he said that this was totally my campaign and he didn't want to get in the way. He suggested that Mr. Pinick, my principal, would be the best person to join me, since he had done so much to get the entire school involved.

The next morning at about 9 A.M., I was in my English class when a small black limousine pulled up to the school to take Mr. Pinick, my parents, and me to the studio. My English teacher, Mr. Barnes, and all of the students in that class came out to see us off. This was an exciting moment, but I was a little nervous and I know Mr. Pinick was as well.

The limo took us to an industrial area, and you would have never guessed what the building was if not for the huge satellite dishes on its side. The studio seemed very small to me; I'm sure it's tiny compared to Fox's studios in Los Angeles or New York. I was amazed at how little the set was. The entire thing was about the size of our dining room, and yet somehow it looked spacious through the camera. One of the things that struck me as funny was the backdrop they used for us. They intended it to look like a library—and it really did on television—but it was nothing more than a painted sheet.

My mom and dad had to wait in an area Fox uses for editing, but were able to watch the interview on a monitor. Meanwhile, while we were getting ready, Fox got a breaking news story and prepared to go live to a news conference as soon as it started. The local producer told my dad that they would cut away from *DaySide* as soon as the news conference began. That would eliminate our spot. Luckily, I didn't know any of this at the time, because I was nervous enough already and would have been even more nervous if I thought there was a chance that we wouldn't get to appear on the show. As it turned out, there was a five-minute delay in the news conference, allowing us just enough time to tell our story to the nation.

Linda Vester, the host of *DaySide*, did her show out of New York in front of a live studio audience. A television interview conducted by someone I couldn't see was a little disorienting. We had to answer as if we were all sitting in the same room, even though we were a continent away from one another. It was the weirdest feeling to answer Linda's questions and then hear my voice in the earpiece delayed a few seconds (something that is standard on live television). I was so tempted to repeat things I'd already said, thinking the words somehow hadn't made it to New York the first time. Back at my school, they watched the interview live in each classroom. I wondered if Mr. Pinick was nervous knowing this was being shown to the entire student population and faculty—but he answered his questions well and I thought he did a great job.

The *DaySide* interview gave "A Million Thanks" a huge boost. That day, the traffic on our Web site became so heavy that people couldn't even get onto it. We logged more than 42,000 Web site hits that day. More than 20,000 came within the hour after the show aired. This was good news and bad news. It was great that we were getting this much attention, but of course I wanted everyone to be able to get through. I could only hope that the people who had trouble connecting would try again later. Meanwhile, my dad went home and checked the e-mail account we'd set up for the campaign. The response was overwhelming. E-mail was coming in so fast that my dad couldn't keep count.

By the end of the day, I had hundreds of e-mail messages to read, from all over the country. There were even some from outside the country. I looked at each message the way a kid looks at a Christmas present, wanting to open it and see what's inside as fast as I could. My dad obviously felt the same way, as he began opening messages as soon as he returned home from the studio.

Unfortunately, one of the messages he opened was from an obviously perverted person. The contents scared my dad so much that he wouldn't let me read it. He called the FBI immediately and faxed the message to an agent in Los Angeles. The agent called back to say they would investigate the message as a possible crime.

When I got home from school later that day, Dad told me about the perverted message and said I could no longer look at new e-mail until he or my mom had looked at it first. He was concerned that, now that I was getting national exposure, I was going to run into a lot of "weirdos." He even went so far as to wonder aloud if everything I was doing was worth being subjected to this kind of thing. I don't think he really meant it; someone saying something awful to me in that message just shook him up. I told him I could take care of myself. After all, I'm a second-degree black belt in Tae Kwon Do. This didn't totally reassure him. We discussed taking extra safety precautions and making sure I didn't walk around anywhere alone. It was a little upsetting to think that some people would abuse what we were trying to do this way, but I wasn't going to let it get to me.

After dinner, I decided that if people took the time to e-mail me, I would take the time to write back. My dad saw me at the computer after 10 P.M. and asked why I was still up. I told him I wanted to answer at least fifty messages a day. He and my mom offered to help but I said I wanted to do it myself, as this was really important to me.

That night, I got a message from Mary S. Most of her spelling was incorrect, but her anguish and sadness came through loud and clear.

Dear Shauna my name is mary s my sonis in afgastion on the front lines.his name is william d. I have ben sick I ned my son home to help me.but the army said no. I have cancer and lung trouble. I am not well. I cry every day every day I miss him so much. my marriage is falling apart. I am so afried william will no come home. we also have Williams 1 cosion in Baghdad right now. Thank you verry much for your help in making our sholders feal better. None of my letters get through to my son I don't hear frome him at all verry much. Thanks a milliomn.

Going through e-mail was a nonstop roller coaster for me. I was excited when I got a message from someone famous, content when someone told me I was making a difference, and devastated when I heard a heart-wrenching story like the one from Mary S. I often felt wrung out at the end of the day, but every ride on this roller coaster strengthened my resolve to fulfill the promise I had made with "A Million Thanks."

Things were quickly moving up to a new level. After the *DaySide* interview, other interview requests started flowing in. Dozens of stations called to discuss my campaign. My absolute favorite interview was on ABC's *World News Now*. I got to go to their big Los Angeles studio for it, and they let me sit at the news anchor desk where Barbara Walters sometimes sits. It made me feel like some big-time newsperson, as opposed to a high school freshman.

Most of my experiences with the media have been positive. The people doing the interviews have for the most part been friendly, attentive, and helpful in getting the story of my campaign out to the public. Some of it has been a little frustrating, though. There have been a few interviewers who have tried to find a "dark side" in my story, or who decided at the last minute not to cover "A Million Thanks" because it was *too positive*. It's like they don't know how to react to something good. The worst of these was a major national talk show (which will remain nameless) that expressed all kinds of interest in doing an interview with me. Then the news about prisoner abuse at Abu Ghraib came out, and suddenly they weren't interested anymore. They actually told us that they thought the encouraging story of "A Million Thanks" would possibly "neutralize" their coverage of the scandal! They were seriously concerned that people would switch from their show to another show while I was on because they wanted more pictures of the prisoners. When things like this happened, I just had to tell myself that the reason was because there was a bigger plan in place, and a more meaningful opportunity around the corner. So far, that has definitely been true.

People often wanted to talk to me first thing in the morning or during school, and Mr. Pinick allowed me to be pulled out of class in the middle of the day—sometimes three or four times in the same day—so I could do these interviews. He knew that we needed this publicity if we were going to get our million letters, and he supported me 100 percent. My teachers were great as well. A few of them teased me about being "a star," but I knew they were on my side. Most of them even took time with me after school when necessary to help me make up any work I'd missed.

My friends were pretty cool about everything that was going on. I know that some of my classmates rolled their eyes when someone from the office came to pull me out, but for the most part I didn't sense any jealousy from anyone or get the sense that anyone thought I was getting preferential treatment. And I really wasn't. I still had to do all of the work that everyone else did, and while it was fun to have someone come to class to let me know that another interviewer was on the line, it was difficult because I wasn't getting the same class time as everyone else. My schoolwork was important to me. I'd always given it 110 percent and got straight A's, and I didn't want to ruin my record. But I had some tough honors classes, and missing class time made them that much tougher.

I could have turned down some of these interviews, but my heart told me this was the wrong thing to do. I felt it was important to take every interview at the beginning, because I wanted to keep the story going. I knew it was the only way to make the campaign as big as it needed to be, and to reach all the soldiers we wanted to reach.

Responding to the daily media calls, answering all of the e-mail, and participating in events related to "A Million Thanks" required making some significant adjustments to my schedule. It felt like I was literally juggling my school responsibilities, my "A Million Thanks" responsibilities, my responsibilities to my softball coaches and teammates, my responsibilities to my family, and my responsibilities to my core group of friends (whom I now almost never got to see). There were times—*lots* of them—when I felt I couldn't keep these balls in the air.

There were also times when I wondered if I had taken on too much with "A Million Thanks." I even occasionally thought about quitting. As exciting as it was, it took up such a huge place in my life that I sometimes wondered if the project was worth it.

Then I would get an e-mail message like this one, from a soldier in Iraq:

Your words of encouragement and the bible verse you sent me made some tears fall. I read it to my soldiers and they were speechless. I want to revert to an old saying . . . whenever you point a finger, four fingers are pointing at you. When I read your e-mail you were pointing your finger at me stating all of the great and wonderful things I'm doing for my country. I'm one of thousands of people trying to make one difference…you're one person making a difference in thousands of soldiers. To my soldiers, your letters build morale. To me, you're building my morale. Thank you again for everything you do for me and the guys. Take care, god bless, and stay sweet.

It's hard to convince myself that my work isn't worth it when I get messages like that. I carry this one and a few others around with me all the time and look at them when I'm feeling tired.

Recently, Kelcie, one of my best friends, shared a Bible verse with me. 2 Corinthians 4:16-18 says, "Therefore we do not lose heart. Though outwardly we are wasting away, yet inwardly we are being renewed day by day. For our light and momentary troubles are achieving for us an eternal glory that far outweighs them all. So we fix our eyes not on what is seen, but on what is unseen. For what is seen is temporary, but what is unseen is eternal."

To me, this captures everything I need to remember about "A Million Thanks." When I feel like things are getting to me, I turn to this verse and it lifts me up, and allows me to run another mile.

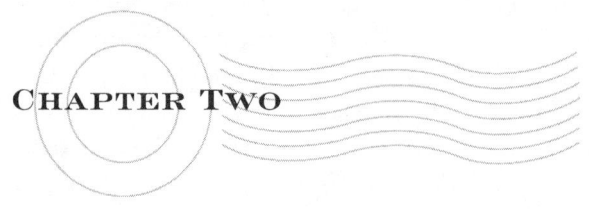

CHAPTER TWO

America Thanks Our Troops

BY THE TIME the letters started pouring in we had a system in place for reading them, sorting them, and getting them out to our soldiers. On April 17, 2004, we held our first biweekly sorting party at the school. This was the Saturday before everyone returned from spring break, and something like forty of my schoolmates had signed up to help. This shocked me because it meant giving up one of the last days of a vacation.

Unfortunately, when we got to school that day, only three of my friends were waiting for us. Eventually about a dozen people came, but it was nowhere near the number we'd expected. I was disappointed, but I think most of them just forgot because they'd been out of classes for a week.

Still, the rest of us had a *big* job to do. We started wheeling the mail from the administration office to the classroom where we were doing the sorting, and I thought, *This isn't going to work.* We had a massive amount of mail and only a handful of us—fueled by the candy, chips, and soda I'd brought—to get through all of it. We had no choice but to make the best of it and get through the piles. The mail was starting to clog up the office hallways, so we really had to get this done.

As I explained to my fellow sorters, we needed to open and review every letter to make sure it was okay to send. Even letters written with the best of intentions had the potential to make a soldier cringe. For instance, a kid could totally innocently say "I hope you don't die" and, while he certainly wouldn't mean anything bad by it, I don't think I'd want to receive that kind of letter if I were fighting in the desert. Once we reviewed the letters, they needed to be bundled in packages of one hundred and placed in boxes.

We got to work and I could see that everyone enjoyed doing this. People constantly stopped to share a letter they'd read, maybe chuckling about something a kid said or showing off an impressive piece of artwork. The time went by amazingly quickly, and even though there weren't as many of us as I'd expected, we made it through all of the mail in record time. We sorted and bundled more than twenty thousand letters in just about two hours.

At the end of this sorting party, we did something that has since become a tradition. Each of us had set aside one letter that made us either laugh or cry, or somehow touched us. Before we left for the day, we took turns reading our letters and then added them to the sorted piles. It was a great way to end the party and it left everyone with a really good feeling.

Just after the *DaySide* broadcast, my dad had told me that the national news would result in a lot of mail. He went to the post office and met the postal manager to tell him what to expect. While they talked, Dad asked about the safety of the mail since it would be coming from all over the country and we'd already learned there were some people out there who weren't so nice. The postal manager told him that the post office had very sophisticated high-tech screening equipment, and that he could rest assured nothing dangerous would get through.

There was one very scary moment, however, during one of the early sorting parties. A bunch of us were working away when one of the kids called my dad over to where he was sorting his letters. He nervously said, "Mr. Fleming, I have something weird here in this envelope." My dad went over and I could see his facial expression change instantly when he looked inside the envelope. The bottom was filled with a white substance. Though my dad didn't say anything to anyone, he told me later that his heart dropped to the floor at that very moment. Not so long before, an anthrax scare had shut down Congress for a day, and anthrax had closed a building in Florida for months. My dad decided to take the envelope and its mysterious contents out of the room while the rest of us stood around, not sure what to do next. If it was anthrax or some other toxic substance, there was a good chance we were already infected.

Outside, Dad gently opened the envelope only to discover a cleverly made card with sugar glued onto it. In transit, most of the sugar had rubbed off and fallen to the bottom of the envelope. He came back in and said, "This is a very sweet card, you guys...lots of sugar!" Everyone laughed, as much out of relief as anything else. The little kid who'd made the card had probably never even heard of anthrax (lucky him!), and had no idea he was going to scare us half to death. Once we knew that the white substance was sugar, we all started breathing again and the rest of the sorting party went off without a hitch.

Word spread quickly about what a great experience the sorting parties were (all sugar aside). Soon we had all the sorters we needed. Some people even started making the parties part of their weekend social plans. This was fortunate, because the flow of mail got very, very heavy for a while.

We even started getting help from outside our school. The president of our key club, a universal service organization, arranged to have key club members from other schools come to sort mail. The day they arrived, I had totally forgotten they were coming. I found something like seventy-five kids waiting for me outside the school, and for a minute I couldn't figure out why they were all there. Then I remembered, and I had to make some quick adjustments. We couldn't have this sorting party in our usual classroom because there were too many kids. We wound up opening mail in the faculty lounge, and still there were people pouring out into the hallways. Because of this, others who happened to walk by decided to join in on the fun. We ordered a bunch of pizzas since I didn't have anywhere near enough snacks. Even with a lunch break, though, we still wound up getting through a mountain of mail in an hour and fifteen minutes. People were actually disappointed that we finished so fast.

There's a great spirit at these sorting parties. While the students who attend get credit toward their community service requirement, most of them don't come for that reason. They come to read the letters and because they know what they're doing makes a difference. Every now and then, I'll read them a letter of thanks from a soldier or soldier's family member to reinforce this point.

We send the boxed letters to bases and camps all across America and wherever our soldiers are stationed overseas. I have also tried to take every opportunity to deliver letters in person when I can.

In July, I visited a place in San Diego where Stu Segall

Productions, the city's only TV and movie studio, simulated an entire Iraqi village for training marines. Stu Segall created and paid for this himself because he felt that, even though our soldiers receive excellent training, nothing in America adequately prepares them for the conditions they will encounter in Iraq. Every single detail in the village was carefully researched and totally realistic—from the Arabic music playing on the streets to actors dressed in authentic Iraqi clothing, from the anti-American messages shouted by the residents to the merchants hiding bombs in fruit in an attempt to kill soldiers. This place was scary. There were goats and other animals roaming around the village, so it smelled like a stable. Explosive experts simulated mortar fire while wound specialists simulated severe field injuries so the marines could learn how to deal with these catastrophes. While I toured the facility, I felt like I was really in Iraq and I got an incredibly strong sense of what our soldiers were going through over there. This is a seriously hostile environment where danger could come from anywhere, even a seemingly friendly face.

When we first walked in, about a hundred soldiers, dressed in full combat gear, were taking a break. They let me hold a gun and try on one of the vests they wore—the ones with pockets everywhere and secret pockets inside of those. The vest must have weighed fifty pounds—and that was on top of the fifteen-pound helmets they all wore. All of this in 100-plus degree weather. Standing there in that simulation of a hazardous Iraqi village, I realized how overwhelming this must be for so many of these soldiers, many of whom were only a few years older than I am.

The captain in charge of the training that day asked me to say a few words to the soldiers. I handed them packets of letters and talked to them about my campaign, telling them how much I appreciated what they were doing. As we talked, the soldiers flipped through the letters. My heart nearly broke as I watched them. These incredibly strong men and women had endured rigorous physical and emotional training. Just minutes before, they'd been prepared to "kill" in order to defend their country and fulfill their mission. They'd been ready to take a bullet for a fellow comrade. Now they had tears in their eyes over something some stranger had written on a sheet of paper. Our sentiments meant that much to them.

I learned just how realistic the village at Stu Segall Productions was when I found out the next day that one of the soldiers in the group I'd spoken to had died when his Hummer rolled over during an exercise. I'd always thought of military training as shooting ranges and obstacle courses, but this was real-life stuff—even under carefully controlled circumstances, the danger was tremendous. It was yet another indication to me of how thankful we should be that anyone would volunteer to go through so much to defend his or her country.

Whenever we attend an event and put up a letter-writing

booth, I talk to people as they write. Those who are most excited by the experience are the kids whose eyes light up as they imagine sending a letter to a real-life version of G.I. Joe. They get even more excited when I tell them that if they include their return address, they might even get a letter back. I can just see them thinking, *G.I. Joe is going to write back to* me? I know that soldiers love having pen pals, and I know they're making a lot of kids happy by doing this. I recently got a great e-mail message from a soldier expressing this very sentiment:

> *I want to let you know about something else your success has done for us that you may or may not know. I've written about 30 people back that left addresses. I received a Thanksgiving card from every one of my AMT (A Million Thanks) pen pals, and not one from my family. I'm sure I'm not the only one here that's had this happen. I just want you to know I had a great Thanksgiving because of AMT.*

Companies and organizations have taken up the cause for "A Million Thanks." Schools and churches and youth organizations have made the letter-writing campaign a group project. One teacher even made the letters part of her English final, instructing her students that they needed to be written in proper letter format. The faculty of a detention center really got into the act, sending us cards awesomely decorated with stickers and even mini-uniforms made out of cloth. The letters in this book are just a small sampling of the extraordinary outpouring I've seen from my fellow Americans. The letters have come from people of all ages and walks of life. For a while we kept track of where the mail was coming from. By the third sorting party, every state in the country was represented. The letters are funny and sad, goofy and heartfelt. What they all have in common, though, is a sincere appreciation for the courage and sacrifice of our military people.

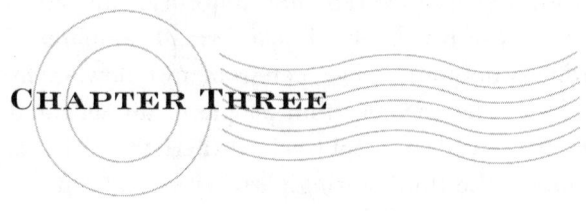

CHAPTER THREE

Hearing Back

BEFORE I BEGAN "A Million Thanks," I told myself that if even one soldier let me know that what I was doing affected him, it would all be worth it. The response from the military, however, has been so much stronger and so much warmer than I ever could have imagined, and I can't even begin to tell you how thrilling that is for me. It makes me feel that this campaign is a good and necessary thing. I am so happy that I can bring even a little light into the lives of these people who are doing so much for us.

Since I began the campaign, I have heard from many soldiers and had the opportunity to learn so much more about what their lives are like. The first soldier I heard from was RP3 Everett Headley, a chaplain's assistant serving with the marines in Iraq. He e-mailed me to thank me for what I was doing, and we began Instant Messaging each other on a regular basis, something we still do today. At first I asked him a lot of questions about the war and his experiences in it, but as time went on, I realized the best thing I could do for him was to take his mind away from this. He sometimes types with very little light and as quickly as he can, so his words and spelling run together. I don't think I could do as well under the circumstances.

AMILLIONTHANKS [8:10 PM]: EV!!!

EVERETTI23 [8:11 PM]: hey!

AMILLIONTHANKS [8:11 PM]: i haven't talked to you in so long, how are you?

EVERETTI23 [8:11 PM]: oh good,
EVERETTI23 [8:11 PM]: tired, hot, but good
EVERETTI23 [8:12 PM]: my life this past month and half is nothing short of a horror movie

AMILLIONTHANKS [8:12 PM]: omg how come?

EVERETTI23 [8:14 PM]: oh yesterday there was a fire fight, i have been mortared and rocketed way too much and ied (improvised explosive devices basically road-side bombs) plague my life

AMillionThanks [8:14 PM]: what's a fire fight?

Everetti23 [8:15 PM]: shooting at each other

AMillionThanks [8:15 PM]: is everything ok? no one got hurt did they?

Everetti23 [8:16 PM]: yes people have gotten hurt

AMillionThanks [8:16 PM]: oh no, that's terrible.... why all of a sudden did they attack?

Everetti23 [8:18 PM]: its not all of a sudden, this has been going on for the past several months. its just as regular as someone throwing a newspaper on your front door step

AMillionThanks [8:18 PM]: how come you haven't told me of this daily stuff before?

Everetti23 [8:19 PM]: because when we talk with the world back home we think of it as an escape from this world and we dont like to dwell on it

AMillionThanks [8:20 PM]: oh im sorry, i didnt mean to bring it up, i just wanted to make sure everything is ok
AMillionThanks [8:20 PM]: what would you like to talk about

EVERETT123 [8:20 PM]: yeah its no problem
EVERETT123 [8:21 PM]: i mean its not a sore subject, but it just happens so often

AMILLIONTHANKS [8:21 PM]: oh, i see
AMILLIONTHANKS [8:21 PM]: what's your favorite movie?

EVERETT123 [8:21 PM]: ya know i have so many i love movies
EVERETT123 [8:22 PM]: but i could watch dumb and dumber over and over

We just continued to talk about "fun stuff," but I knew that after we were done, I'd get to go downstairs and watch TV, while Ev would go to his office not knowing if rockets or bullets were going to end his life that day.

AMILLIONTHANKS [11:18 AM]: How are you?

EVERETT123 [11:19 AM]: good
EVERETT123 [11:19 AM]: i just moved from fallujah
EVERETT123 [11:19 AM]: and reached my highest temp yet of 132

AMILLIONTHANKS [11:19 AM]: Wow! Where did you move to?

AMillionThanks [11:19 AM]: Anything new going on?

Everett123 [11:20 AM]: mahmadiyah, sixteen miles south of baghdad
Everett123 [11:20 AM]: nope , sorry to say, same old war

Ev is in the navy. He's the first member of the military I mention when interviewers ask me about the people I've met and the impact they've had on me. I consider Everett to be a friend even though we've never met, and he has taught me things about military life that I only had vague ideas about before.

AMillionThanks [9:21 PM]: what are you doing today?
AMillionThanks [9:21 PM]: or in my case, tomorrow?

Everett123 [9:21 PM]: umm
Everett123 [9:21 PM]: taking a nap
Everett123 [9:21 PM]: walking around talking to my marines
Everett123 [9:21 PM]: i am going to talk to the guys who disassemble bombs today

AMillionThanks [9:22 PM]: what do you talk to them about?

AMILLIONTHANKS [9:22 PM]: or do you just hang out

EVERETT123 [9:23 PM]: i just hang out and let them talk, decompress we like to say so that they can get stuff off their chest
EVERETT123 [9:23 PM]: i am there to help them know everything is ok and life gets better

One day, Everett gave me a real scare. I had started doing a monthly radio show on wsRadio.com, the largest Internet radio network in the world, run by Chris Murch, a highly decorated former marine. Everett was going to be the first active soldier ever to appear on my new show. This was very exciting.

My dad was working the phone board for me and it was getting close to the time for Everett to call in. The board was in another room, and the wall between my dad and me had a large window so we could see each other. Chris Murch was at my side to guide me along, because the show was airing live and I was still pretty new to all of this.

As the time to interview Ev approached, my dad shook his head to let me know he hadn't called in yet. Ev and I had spoken the night before, so I knew he knew the schedule. I bumped all my interviews up one. As each interview went on, I waited anxiously for Ev to call in. Still there was nothing. Finally, the show ended with no word from him. All kinds of thoughts ran through my mind. I had no idea if he was okay or if he was in trouble, or worse.

Later that afternoon my dad learned that there had been a series of bombings in Baghdad, and that several marines had died in the area near Ev. I e-mailed Ev a couple of times and he didn't respond. I began to fear the worst. It was at this point that I started to understand how it must feel to have a family member or friend missing at war with no word of their fate. I felt awful. My stomach was an empty pit. All I could think about was Ev. All of the "what ifs" filled my head. I can't imagine how people go through this all the time when their loved ones are off fighting.

Two days went by. Finally, I got an e-mail from Ev! He told me that just ten minutes before the interview, his unit was mortared and all power had to be shut down, including the phone. This really drove home for me just how perilous the life of a soldier is, how quickly things can go wrong, and how much bravery is required just to get through the day.

A call from Private First Class Michael Byrd of the 112th 1st Calvary Division in Iraq reinforced for me this sense of peril. It was about three in the morning (his time) when he called to thank me for what I was doing. One of the first things he said to me was, "Don't worry if you hear some explosions in the background. We get mortared around this time every day."

"That must be incredibly dangerous," I said. "Aren't you worried?"

"Nah, they always miss. We get mortared three times every day—once in the morning, once in the evening, and once in the middle of the night—and they never hit us. We take precautions, but I'm not worried."

He seemed totally casual about this, but it seemed very scary to me. Even if the Iraqis *always* missed, wasn't there still a chance they could hit at some point, even accidentally? Because of the nature of the phone equipment, there was a delay of several seconds between each exchange, and I kept wondering during these delays if something had happened on his end. Knowing I was going to be bombed three times a day would have driven me crazy, but Michael kept his cool, acting like it was just another thing going on in his life.

Over Memorial Day weekend, I got to meet with some of the soldiers from the 82nd Airborne in Charlotte before the Coca-Cola 600 NASCAR race. This gave me another glimpse of what life is like at war. Many of these guys had already been to Iraq and would be going back again in a couple of months. One of the soldiers, Ryan Curry, let me hold his gun and I asked him what it was like to be over there. I asked him if he'd ever killed anyone. I wouldn't usually ask this kind of question because of the terrible memories it brings to the surface, but for some reason I felt like I could ask Ryan.

"I've killed a few people during combat."

"Wow, how did that feel? Do you feel guilty or sad when you do something like that?"

"Not when it's happening. When someone has a gun pointed at you and you know he wants to kill you, you don't feel bad about pulling the trigger. Afterwards, though, I think about it and it starts to get to me."

Again, the reality of what these people face when they're over there hit home for me. Of all the soldiers I've spoken to, this one had seen the most hardcore action, but there are plenty of other people just like him, men and women challenged on a constant basis by a dangerous and often unseen enemy. People who regularly have to choose to kill or be killed. That our soldiers have faced these conditions throughout American history is amazing to me when I compare it to the easy lives most of us have. We can never show enough appreciation for the sacrifice necessary to do what these people do.

It seems unbelievable to me that soldiers would ever consider what I was doing to be impressive, but on my trip to Charlotte this message came through loud and clear. I met Dennis Lee Cavin, a three-star general, who presented me with a Coin of Excellence as a way of showing his appreciation for "A Million Thanks." He said that very few people got the coin, and almost all of the recipients were members of the army. He felt, though, that my campaign made a real contribution toward maintaining morale among the troops and so I deserved to have one. This amazed me. I could barely believe it when he handed me the coin.

The surprises weren't over on this trip. As I started to leave with my family, Major Fred Rice and Major Paul Stamps came running up to me. They said they were glad to catch me because they didn't want me to go before they presented another army coin. This one was the Coin of Army Values. On the back, it listed the core values of a serviceman: loyalty, duty, respect, selfless service, honor, integrity, and personal courage. I thought it was just incredible that they were willing to give one to me, but they told me they thought I deserved it for everything I was doing. This touched me deeply. It was a moment I'll remember my entire life. Then, to top it off, Major Stamps asked me *for my autograph*. I thought he was kidding and I laughed, but he handed me a piece of paper and asked me to sign it, and I could tell he was serious. I gave them both hugs and told them I would never forget them, and hoped our paths would cross again soon.

While I'd had e-mail and phone contact with soldiers before this, and met numerous soldiers at the USO and March Air Force Base, this trip to Charlotte took the experience to another level entirely and made me even more committed to "A Million Thanks." At one point while we were there, something like a hundred army members, including the 82nd Airborne Chorus, surrounded me. They were so thrilled with what I was doing and told me how much letters from the public meant to them. It became obvious to me that these men and women, who are so strong in who they are, and who exhibit extraordinary levels of bravery performing their duty, feed off our support. They are able to be as brave as they need to be and overcome some incredibly scary situations because they know that their country believes in them, and that we appreciate everything they're doing for us. I left Charlotte with the strongest sense yet that we needed to touch as many of these people's lives with "A Million Thanks" as we possibly could.

In addition to the soldiers I've met over the course of this campaign, I've had contact with a number of people who have loved ones serving in Iraq. They, too, have given me a new perspective on the sacrifice and determination required by everyone involved in defending our country.

Dear Shauna,

This is my son. [Attached was a photo of him in Iraq sitting on top of a Humvee and holding a mounted machine gun.] *He is my only child. He joined the ARMY NATL GUARD at 17 & he spent his 20th b-day in northern Iraq on May 3rd, 2004. Because of security reasons, the actual destination cannot be disclosed. I am writing to THANK YOU for what you are doing. My son is the type of person—well—that you just can't but adore. He has done more in the last couple of years than most people will do in a lifetime.*

When the issue of going to Iraq came up—as a parent I wanted nothing to do with this—I wanted him to stay home. My son on the other hand had no reservations whatsoever. He said, "Mom, I finally get to do what I was trained to do." With that, I left it alone. I would never disrespect him by trying to stop him after those comments. I had a chance to meet with some of his fellow soldiers in his unit. They are some of the finest individuals you would ever meet. They are proud and stern with their beliefs and at the same time the most humble group of people. They have a job to do and they are going to do it, then they will come home!!! I have no doubt that they will keep each other safe—they are family!!!

So for my son and his unit, I again thank you. 276 Engineer Battalion Charlie Company somewhere in Northern Iraq.

Sincerely,

a mother of an American soldier

I recently received an Instant Message from her son, David. He thanked me for the box of mail I sent him and for the good work I have been doing. We've started to correspond regularly.

The following e-mail message touched me incredibly deeply, as I'm sure it would anyone who received something like it:

Dear Shauna,

Someone I work with told me about your website. I went to it and my heart was touched by what you are doing. My nephew was killed in Iraq on April 6, 2004. We are heartbroken but we will come to a place where we can heal because we knew he was doing what he wanted to do and that God has a plan for all of us.

Christopher was not much older than you, just graduated high school last May, and he would be very proud to know that one person like you could make such a huge difference to help his fellow comrades who are still over in Iraq fighting for our freedoms. He was very concerned about the safety of the others in his unit and all who are fighting. My sister received a letter from him just the other day (probably the last one he wrote to her) and in it he vowed that he would protect himself and the others he was with and would come home himself. Sadly, God had other plans and will use Christopher's memory to work through others. It is already happening in our community.

We have come to realize that while our grief has touched our lives with such tremendous force, there are many, many other families that are going through the same thing, and many, many other families who have someone over there, still fighting but needing to know that they are supported by people back home. So thank you for what you are doing and I will send your website to others.

God bless,
Pamela M.

It took me a while to recover after reading that one, but at the same time it reinforced my belief in what I was doing and what we all need to do, not only for our soldiers but also for those at home who love them. After all, if the families of military people see and feel our support, they might deal with the fear and worry they must experience every single day just a little bit better.

Recently, I met the marketing noncommissioned officer for the National Guard and its NASCAR team, Sergeant First Class John Metzler. He has been with the Guard for nineteen years. I went to the SpeedFreaks Radio pre-race party (for the Pop Secret 500 at nearby California Speedway in Fontana) at his invitation. The whole night, he kept telling me how much what I was doing meant to him. He introduced me to everyone there as the "A Million Thanks girl." We were supposed to leave around nine because I had school the next morning, but as we walked out to our car, we got into another long conversation and I suddenly had no desire to go.

He told me that he'd decided to nominate me as an American Home Front Hero, an honor the National Guard bestows upon civilians who perform special service in support of our military. He told me that each member of the army can nominate only one Home Front Hero throughout his entire career, and that of all the people he'd encountered as a soldier, he'd chosen me. A whole bunch of emotions welled up inside me. He hadn't even met me in person when he'd nominated me.

"You don't get it, do you?" he said when I told him how surprised and honored I felt by this. "You think you know what you have done for these men, but you have no idea."

I felt I had a slightly better idea when he gave me the biggest hug and I looked into his eyes. It seems curious that in only one night, someone could change a life, but that was the case for me. I replayed that night over and over again in my mind, continually thinking of what John had told me.

The intention of "A Million Thanks" was always to reach out to all military personnel, both active and retired. In late June, my dad and I visited Veterans Administration Hospital in Westwood, one of the largest VA hospitals in the country. This was my first visit to a VA hospital, so I really didn't know what to expect. I saw patients walking around the grounds and commented to my dad that they looked okay to me. Some used canes, walkers, and wheelchairs, but most looked fine. My dad said, "They're okay *physically*, but a lot of them have been scarred mentally and emotionally." In fact, so many of the people we met that day had been through terrible things in Korea and Vietnam, things that left their bodies healthy, but affected their minds in ways from which they will never recover.

I remembered the stories I'd heard about the reception soldiers received when they returned from Vietnam, how people called them horrible names and spit at them and shunned them. Knowing what I know now about what soldiers go through, how important public support is to their psyches—and how desperately they need that support in order to do what we've sent them to do—I wished I could go back in time to do something like "A Million Thanks" in the sixties and early seventies. How much different would the lives of these men be today if we could have let them know—regardless of our feelings about the war—that we appreciated their sacrifice and what they were doing for our sake?

Every soldier I've met and corresponded with has had a huge impact on me. I've always had respect for people who served their country, but now that I've gotten to know many of them and learn a little bit about what they experience, that respect has increased a thousand times. With this greater respect has come a deeper understanding of why I was called to do "A Million Thanks." As incredibly small as my contribution seems to me to be, I understand how valuable it is for every military person—whether in Iraq or here, whether active or retired—to hear that he or she is appreciated.

I recently spoke to a soldier who had just come back from the war. He told me that his unit got regular drop-ships of all sorts of supplies—food, toiletries, books, DVDs, etc. When the boxes were dropped, he and his friends would tear them apart looking for one thing—mail. None of the other stuff was anywhere near as important to them as letters from home.

"This is our gold," he told me. With every passing day, with every soldier I meet, I understand what he meant a little bit more.

Dear soldier,

Thank you for going to the war and doing your job. You have saved our lives. I know it's a difficult job but you do great. You have saved us from getting killed. You are very generous for trying to save us and George W. Bush. I'm sure he's proud.

Your grateful friend

Nicholas   Age 9

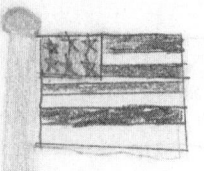

Fullerton California

Jackson ville NC

Dear Troop,

Hi, How are you? Hopefully good, given the circumstance's. I know its odd reading a letter from a stranger so I'll give you a little info about myself.

I come from a bit of a military family. My father was in, my sister-in-law, my husband's father, and my husband and brother are currently active duty waiting to be re-deployed themselves. I myself went to bootcamp for the Marines last summer (2005) but after 6 mo. I got a medical discharge due to an injury during training.

Having you guys over there means alot to me personally because I also have loved ones fighting along side of you. There are many times I've seen things in the media and it makes me cry knowing that more troops will be deployed and many returns back home. Both with sadness and joy.

Know though that you and everyone over there are appreciated and loved. My prayers are with you.

Always-
Amber

Dear Military Personnel,

I'm writing you to thank you for all of your dedication and the sacrifices that you have made for us. Your dedication to the military has made a difference in my life as well as many others. To devote your life to fighting for others is "awesome" and deserves a thanks; having to sacrifice everything to fight for someone else's freedom deserves a thanks. Giving up your life with your family and friends is a big decision to make on others' behalf. I appreciate everything you do, "keep fighting the good fight."

Proud American,

Brittany

To our brave troups:

We are without adequate words to describe our gratitude to each of you for the incredible sacrifice, Continuing effort, and overwhelmingly difficult job each of you has. We are continuously aware of your work and are amazed, again and again, of and how dedicated you are to the task at hand and our Country as a whole. We pray for all of you ~ first, for your safety. We hope and wait anxiously for your return to the States. Secondly, that you may never lose sight of the goal ~ our continued freedom. And thirdly, for your strength. The daily stress you face goes far beyond what we can imagine and we are strongly aware that what we do, safe on our streets and in our homes, can in no way, compare to the dangers you face.

Pg 2

We want you to know that you are indeed
valued and remembered for everything you
have sacrificed and continue to sacrifice on
our behalf. Our children, Kiren, Joshua, Caleb,
and soon to arrive, Judah, will know what
freedom means because of the efforts you make
today.

With our love & continued prayers,

Dave and Koa

Placentia CA

To all Service Men and Women,

Just a note to try and express my appreciation and gratitude to all of you for the service and sacrifice you are giving to your country and to me. I keep all of you in my prayers and hope that you will be able to come home soon. I am so proud of all of you for your commitment to keep our nation safe. It seems we live in such a selfish world today and I am amazed at the number of young men and women who are willing to give so much for others. I for one appreciate it greatly and wanted to let you know. I will continue to pray and hope that this conflict will end soon, I pray for our country leaders that they will make wise choices, I pray for your families who I know miss you immensely, and mostly for you.

Thank you again for all you do and have done. I am proud of you and wish you Godspeed.

Sincerely yours,

Linda

Linda

Marysville, Oh

McNeill, ms

Dear Military Personnel,

I am taking the time to write an appreci-ation letter to you. Thank you for Serving overseas and keeping not only our country Safe, but other countries as well. I think you are God's gift from heaven sent down to protect the United States from terrorists.

I want to follow in my brother's footsteps and become a Navy Seal one day. I know you would like to come home and we want you to. We really thank you for giving your time. Hopefully one day the entire world will be free.

Thanks Sincerely,
Kenny

Carriere, Mississippi

Dear Military Personnel,

Hey, my name is Brett. I am in tenth grade.

I enjoy playing guitar and piano. I also love playing sports, but have no time to do so at school.

Now that I have told you a little about myself, I will get to the main objective of my letter. I want to tell you thank you for your part in ensuring my freedom. I cannot explain how much I appreciate your willingness to risk your life to protect mine. Keep up the good work, and God Bless!

Sincerely,
Brett

P.S. Write back if you would like.

Dear Soldier,

Though we do not know each other and may never meet, I want you to know that I am one of thousands of Americans who are praying for you and thinking of you daily as you serve. These are difficult days and I can only imagine the trials you are facing. As you deal with a variety of emotions and challenges, I am asking God to lift you up and encourage you in the midst of it all.

Each night when I tuck my children in bed, our prayers are for your protection and for your success. We pray that you will return home safe and want you to know that you are deeply appreciated. Our prayers will continue as long as you serve.

God has blessed our nation with an incredible freedom that comes at an incredible price. Your part in paying that price, as you give up so much of your freedom, is something I will never take for granted or forget. As a Christian, I am reminded that Jesus Christ counted the cost of a great battle before He went to the cross to die for our sins. The power of His choice has offered spiritual freedom for the whole world. If you do not know Christ as your Savior, He is there for you right now and you can ask Him to be your Savior in the privacy of your heart. He has promised to help all those who seek Him and make our hearts right because of His work on the cross. Pray to Him anytime and He will hear you.

As a Pastor of a church in California, I will continue to have our congregation pray for you and those you serve with. Thank you again for what you do and contact me if I can pray for anything specific for you.

God bless you and keep you safe!

Pastor Mark

Mu Iota Chapter  **University of Kentucky**

Alpha Tau Omega

To the Defenders of our Freedoms:

Thank you for your valuable service that you provide to our country. We do not forget that everyday you stand up for what all of us believe in and cherish. Without you, we could not enjoy the security we have always known. We do not take for granted what your effort and courage provide to us. We have many brothers there among you, and we wish well to everyone. Thank you for continuing fighting for our freedoms and our way of life.

With Great Respect,

The Brothers of Alpha Tau Omega

Middlesboro ky,

Dear Soldier,
Who fights for freedom who
defends there country it's you soldier. You
the unafraid american, You the brave fearless
courageous daring hero. I ment that
too. I am very grateful for what you
are doing for this brave country. S
thank you you brave soul. I am writing
to you because I want to thank you
for all the work you have done
for the past year or 2 years. So
heres all of my thanks thank you
everybody
A 4th grade american,
Coddie
Ps. write me back on this
please

Bill   Kelly   Matt   Aubrey   Carlisle   Delaney

Dear Soldier,

Hi, my name is Kelly. I'm the mother of 4! My son, Matt is 12, my daughters are Aubrey @ 10, Carlisle @ 7 & Delaney is the baby @ 4 yrs. My husband Bill works for Hewlett-Packard in Austin, TX.

There's no way I can really thank you for what you're doing for us by serving our country. Please know that I pray for you daily.

I watch my kids & know that there are mothers in Iraq & Afganistan who are watching their children play & go to school for the first time.

You are standing firm & bringing freedom to people who would have never known it. You are changing lives for generations & generations. That's pretty wild if you think about it.

Thank you for all your sacrifices on behalf of your country & its people. I also thank your families for all they are sacrificing.

I have a special place in my heart for military families

because I'm from one.
My Dad is a retired Colonel.
He served 30 years + 2 stints
in Vietnam. We moved almost
every year. One year we
moved 3 times!

I understand the unique
stresses that military families
have. I also relish the
opportunities I had to travel,
see different places+ meet
lots of people + be part of something
bigger then most.

The patriotism, concern for
others, loyalty, trust + don't
forget discipline I learned
from my father + his career.
are hopefully being passed on
to my kids.

Thank you again for all you
do + all you stand for. You
should be very proud of your
choices.

Sincerely
Kelly

Dear military Men and Women,

My name is Josh. At school I have band and chorus as my special classes. I live in Westminster M.D. I have one brother and one sister. I'm the middle kid. I like sports and vidio games just like any other kid. I play soccer, baseball and basketball. I'm in fourth grade and I have A's and B's in all of my classes. The chorus tryouts were not to long ago and I made it. My granpa was in the Korean War.

Now you know something about me now I want to tell you all how much we all appreciate you. I want to thank you for protecting our country. I hope you come home safe. I want to thank you for risking your lives to save our country. You are doing a great job protecting the U.S.A. You are doing so much I don't know how I can repay you.

here is me →

Sincerely,
Josh

Please write back to me.

West, MD.

Dear Servicemember,

Thanks for doing all that stuff for our country, I really appreciate it. I hope you guys come back home to tell your really cool story! :-)

Sincerely,
CJ

P.S. Write back if you can!

CJ

Anahiem Hills
CA

THANKS

AGAIN

Dear Soldier,

thank you!
I bet your
wondering
why I'm say-
-ing thank You.
well du its
for saveing our
cuntry.

Plese write
back
I hope
you come
Back
Soon!
with hope
from Courtney

U.S. Soldier,

We wanted you to know that you are thought of often. We do appreciate your willingness to serve our Country. We support you 100%! We know there are many sacrifices you have made. My brother was involved with Desert Shield and was stationed in Saudi Arabia for a while. We were very proud of him and his efforts he had made to accomplish that task at hand. He now works for the Air Force as a civilian and loves his job (he does polygraphs....says he can't divulge exactly what he does). He has some really surprising stories, as I am sure you do too. Whether you are near the front, on the front, or doing support in the background, we are very proud of you and all you do! We know freedom doesn't come free! Without you we would not have the safe haven we experience today here in the U.S. Some people truly take advantage of what you all are doing for us. However rest a sure, my family does not! May God continue to be with you and your family. May He watch over you! You are all in our prayers.

Julie

San Jose, CA

Dear soldier,

Thank you for serving our country in the military. Also I thank you for your bravery and for fiting for the Uited States we appreciate for what you do for us. I feel sad for you that you have to do that for us.

I am a sixth grader. I now you feel my cousen is in the army to. I live with my father, mother, brother and me.

from,
Anthony

orange county california

Dear Serviceperson:

Hello, hello. I'm writing to you to thank you from the bottom of our hearts for your sacrifice.

I would like you to know that there are a lot of Americans who not only support you, but pray for your safe return to your homes.

There are too many Americans who don't realize that everything they have is because of people like you who are protecting their rights and their loved ones.

The only appropriate words are THANK YOU.

Thank you for protecting us, and God Bless you all.

Terri & Lou
Commerce, California

```
   ~
  \o/
  / \
   "
```

Monday, May 03, 2004

Dear Soldier,

My class and I would like to thank you for all you do to
protect our country in these uncertain times. It is hard
being out of the country and away from your family.
Just know your efforts are appreciated by millions even
though they may not take the time to express their
appreciation. God bless you and we are praying for your
safety and safe return to the best country (because of
you) in the world, the USA!!!

In Christ,

Mrs. Ann

Mrs. Ann
First Grade Teacher
St. John Lutheran School

Williamsburg, Ky

Dear Military Personnel,

Hello! My name is Tiffany

It's weird knowing that in
just a few, short weeks many of
my class mates will be enrolled
in some military program, fighting
for the lives of innocent people.
To me the military is the most
honorable duty anyone can serve.
It takes a lot of heart, and
courage to get out there and fight
for your country. I think I can
speak for most people when I say
we appreciate everything that you
are doing for our country, and
that not a day goes by when I
don't pray for you all.
You all are truely an insperation
to us all. Keep up the good

Work and this will all be over
soon, hopefully.

P.S. Included is a picture of my
class and write back soon. I
would love to know who I've
wrote to, please.

Best of Luck,
Tiffany

Dear Service Person —

I am so pleased to be One-in-A Million, as part of the A Million Thanks program. We appreciate the sacrifices that you are enduring and you are not forgotten. This effort (A Million Thanks) is one of many in which we Americans Stateside try to show our appreciation.

I believe that what you have been asked to do has value. Your efforts will be rewarded. You are making a difference. We are insanely proud of our people in uniform. They represent us — you represent us — and you do it well. I can't help but believe that what you are doing and how you are doing it, will change the course of history.

I am proud to be an American, and very proud of you — our personal representative. Thank you so much.

Regards,
Annette

Dear Military Service man,

My Name is Daniel . I libe in Corona, CA. I have lived here all my life and enjoy Californias moderate weather.

I thank you for what you are doing for me and the United States. I think that you are a hero in my eyes for you have been in Iraq for a while and you have made a sacratice for us. I will be looking forward to the day that you and every one of the people serving in Iraq come back to the United States.

We willatl be glad when you all come home safely. I have 3 friends that are over in Iraq and one more in the reserve. I hope this is resolved quickly.

God's Speed,

Daniel

Dear Solider,

My name is Breanna and I am 17 years old. I live in modesto California.

I appreciate all you have done and will do for our country. You are an inspiration to me and people I know. I am glad you are helping the Iraqgwies. I would like to know what you are doing there! I am intrested in knowing about you and all that you have accomplished. Please write back to:

Breanna

P.S. If you know a Seth tell him I said Hi! Thanks and may God Bless!

GOD Bless America and All of YOU!

Honey Bear & Muffin

Dear special Friend,
Thank you so much for doing many things for our nation. May God keep you safe and bless you! My class and I will pray for you!

Love,
Angeline

To alot of people this picture just means a bunch of rumble, jumble, but to me it's a sign of dignity, freedom, justice, sacrifice, honor, and bravery. So thank you so very much for taking the chance to lose your life to save mine. My uncle was also in the military. If you know him you might know him as Randy or Blake.

I'll pray for you. God Bless you. May God have his hand on you and your family.

Santa Maria, CA

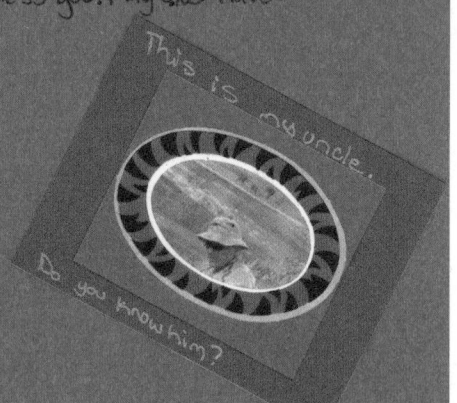

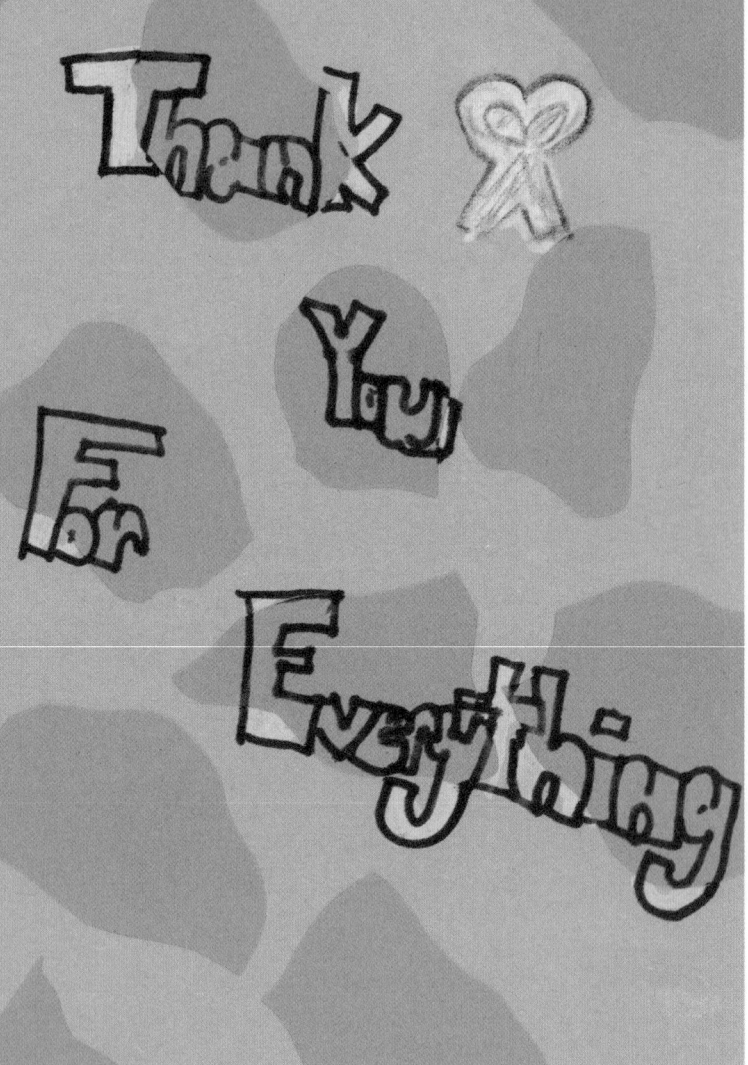

Dear Soldiers,

Thank you for making me feel safe. Thank you very much for doing that.

Much Thanks,
Anjali

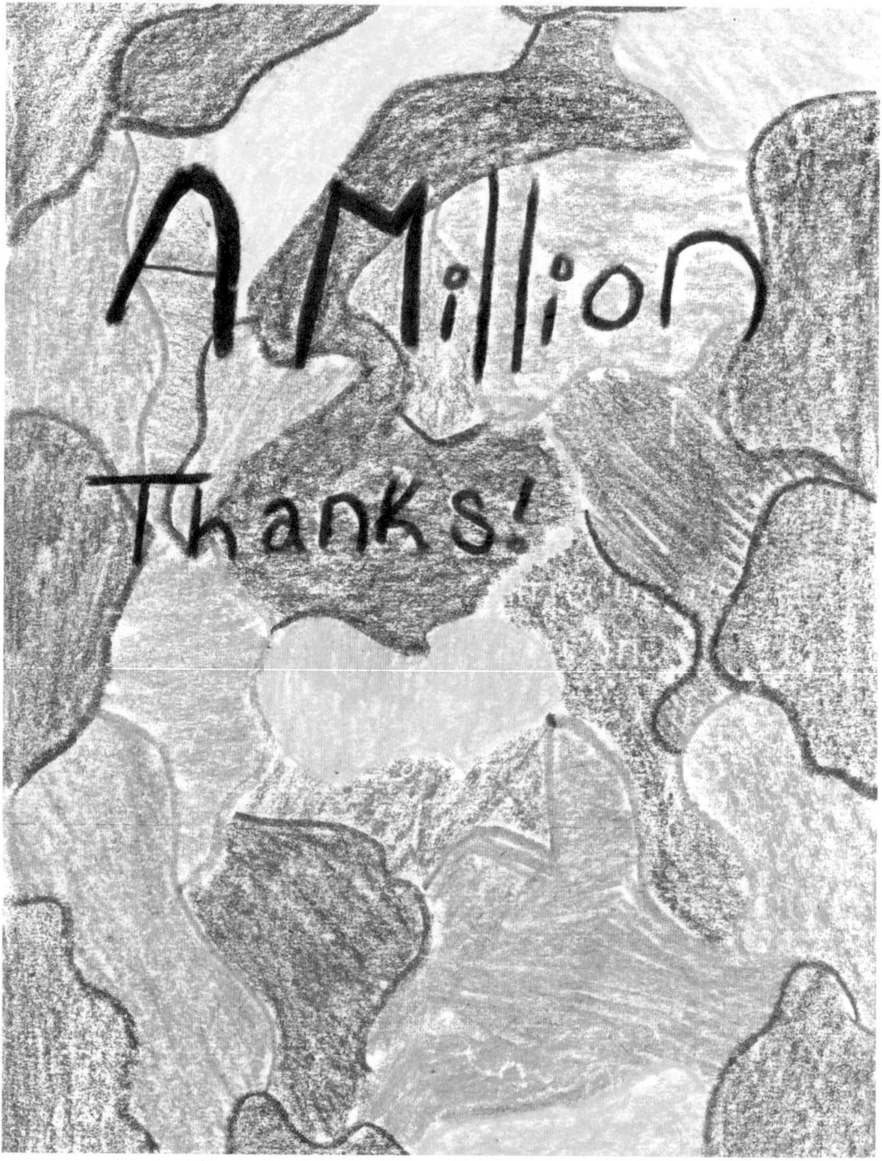
A Million
Thanks!

Dear U.S. Military Person,

Thank you for doing the things you do. I'm glad to say this card is for you. I couldn't imagine the things you must have to cope with. Please write back,

In Christ,
andy

God bless you

God makes
a wish come
true love

bring LOVE
Us
Soldiers
home

U.S. Soldier,

Hi my name is Brent.   I am in the 4th grade. I like to play soccer. I am on a competitive team. We played in a tournament last Sunday. We won 1, lost 2, and tied 2. I have a puppy named Annie (as you can see). She is a really good dog. She likes to chase shadows and wrestle a lot. We got her when she was 5 weeks old and was as small as a genie pig. Now look at her! I have a lot of fun with her. How are you doing? My class is sending care packages with the Red Cross for you guys. Maybe you will get one? My brother and I made a sign that says, "honk for America". We stand on our street corner. Lots of people are honking for you. We support you! Thank you for all you do.

Brent

San Jose, CA

United We Stand !!

I pledge my heart to the United States OF America

Hello From Salem. Mo,
Thank you for all that
You do & I'm thinking
of you.

Love,
Love,
Sauhanna

Dear Serviceman,

We are so proud of you! We want you to know that we have been praying for you continually. You are such brave men in wanting to protect us from harm. In the Bible in Proverbs 3:5,6 it says: "Trust in the Lord with all your heart and lean not on your own understanding; in all your ways acknowledge Him, and he will make your paths straight.

Tim and Jean
San Diego, CA

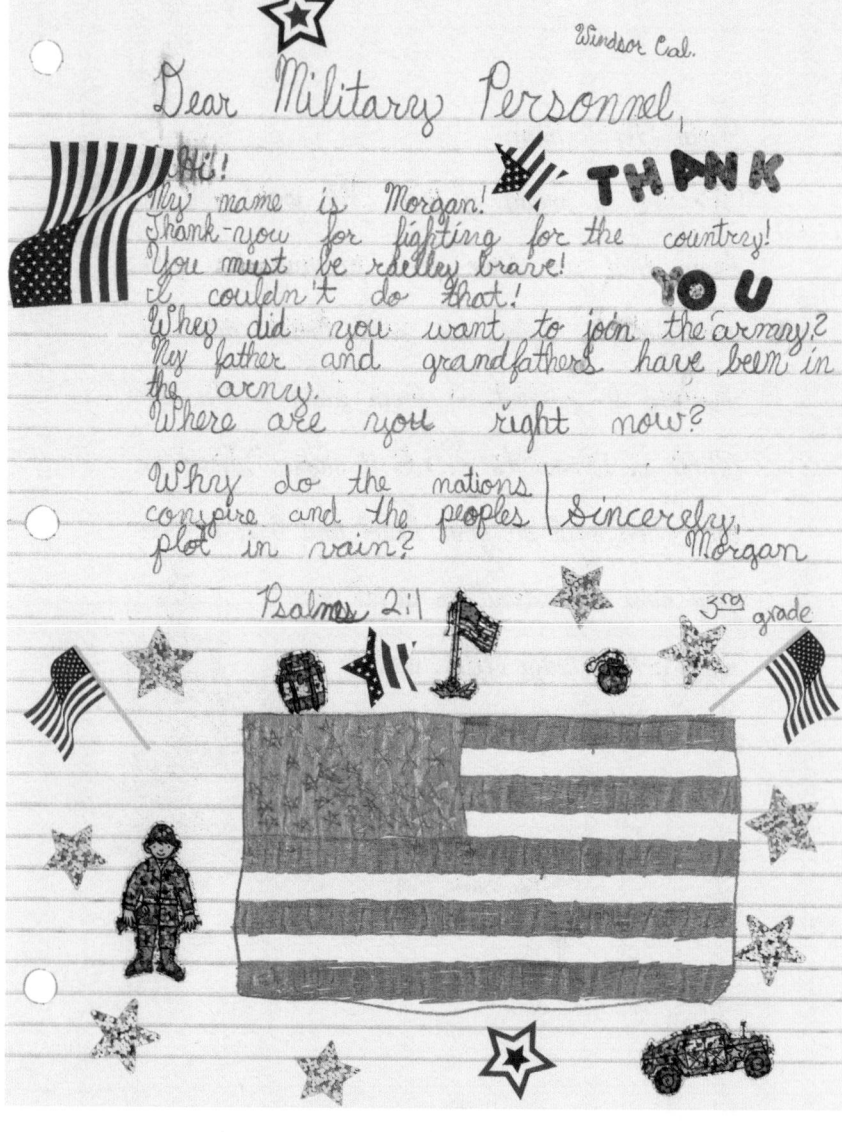

Windsor Cal.

Dear Military Personnel,

Hi!
My name is Morgan!
Thank-you for fighting for the country!
You must be reelley brave!
I couldn't do that!
When did you want to join the army?
My father and grandfathers have been in the army.
Where are you right now?

Why do the nations conspire and the peoples plot in vain?

THANK YOU

Sincerely,
Morgan

Psalmes 2:1

3rd grade

Dear Soldiers,

I am a 4th grade student in Laguna Niguel, California. I would like to extend my sincere appreciation to you and your families for protecting our country. Thank you very much for your courage, sacrifice and patriotism so we can have normal life at home. I'll take my responsibility like you to continue to be a straight A student. When I grow up, I'll be ready to serve our country.

Have a good Easter and best luck to you!

Love,
Charles

Thanks so much for what you are doing. I don't know what I would be doing or where I would be if it was not for what you are doing. I hope it isn't that bad for you where you are at. My hopes, prayers and good thoughts go to you. Well it would be nice to get a letter back from you maybe telling me whats going on or maybe you just want to tell someone somethings that are on your mind. I am a freshman in High School and live in Orange County.

Sincerly,
Kesley

Tustin, CA

US Soldier,

Hi, my name is Matthew, I am 12 and in the sixth grade. I wanted to thank you for fighting for our country. My family supports you guys 120%! My brother and I like to stand in front of our house with a sign that says "Honk for the troops at war." We also went to a support our troops rally. There was one guy in his truck that went by us every 5min, just so he could honk!! I know Freedom **DOESN'T COME FREE**. I just want to thank you again for all that you do. I know there are a lot of sacrifices you have had to make, but keep up the good work!! Thanks a million!!!

Matthew

San Jose CA

Me Holding flag

my brother saluting

Huntington Beach, CA
4th grade rm 26

To our troops;
Thank you for fighting for our country and keeping peace in Iraq. It must be hard. Thanks again.

Sincerely,
Daniel

Dear Soldier,

My name is Amber and three of my favorite colors are pink, black, & red. My hair is blonde, I have green eyes and also glasses & braces and my ears are pierced, I am 11 years

Thank you for protecting us. I really apricate all of you and all of your hard work. Please keep me safe and all of you to, so please keep trying. Thank you for serving.

Sincerely,
Amber

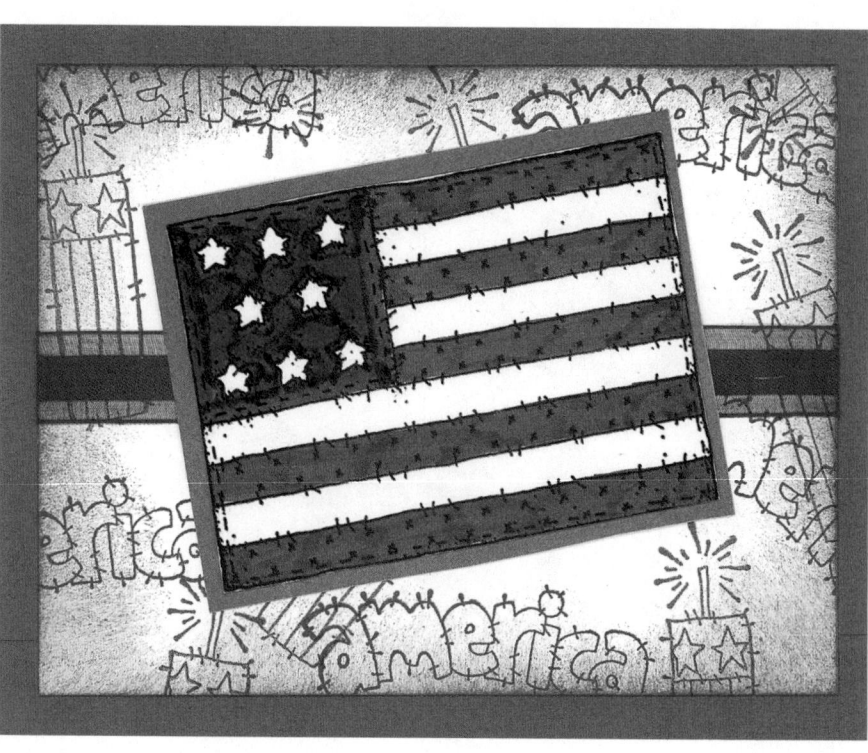

Dear Friend,

I wanted to take this opportunity to say thank you for your dedication and service to your country. I know it's probably not much with just a card, but I just wanted you know that I and many many others are praying for you. Wherever you go and whatever you do we are proud of you.

If you would like to write back, I'll write back to you. Stay safe!

All my prayers

Barbara

 WE LOVE YALL AMERICA

Thank you for your dedication and bravery. Because of you + your troops my children are safer and can grow up in a free nation. Keep your head held high! God bless you + your family. Ya'll are in our prayers daily!

Sincerely
Tom + Robin
& family

Mandi - 19
Ben - 16
Casey - 15
Brenna - 12

. . . so much for everything! We all are very grateful! God bless you!

always,

Ruth

 I love frogs

Hey,

I am Carissa and I am a freshman in High School. Our whole class is writing letters. I want you to know that I think it is great that you are in Iraq fighting for our country!! My brother use to be in Iraq but he allready came home! I was so happy when I saw him. I just hope you know that we all appreciate what you are doing over there. Today it is the 20th of may and I am not sure when you will get this but I was wondering if you would write back to me. But if you dont I will understand. I think it would be great to be able to write to you back and forth. Well I don't know what else to say right now because you haven't wrote me at all. So here is my address if you want to write back. And Take Cair of yourself!!
   Carissa

A fellow American,
   Carissa

Sorry I might be bad at spelling!
                    he he he

Dear John/Jane Doe,

I am a fourteen-year-old girl from Green Bay, Wisconsin who has decided to take part in writing on of the one million letters that are going to be sent to soldiers overseas, such as yourself. My name is Lindsay   , and I am going to be a freshman next year   as of now, I am an eighth grader   but by the time you get this letter, the school year will most likely be over (Thank goodness).

There is really no way to express the way I feel about the conflicts going on outside the United States, mainly the War in Iraq. I feel confused about what's going on because, no matter how much I read or hear about the War, I don't fully understand anything about what's going on. Does anyone who has never taken part in war understand it? Along with not understanding, I also have all of these jumbled emotions bouncing around inside me; it's kind of like I don't know how to feel about what's going on in our world. That doesn't make much sense, does it?

How do you feel about all of this? You obviously feel something about what is going on, or you wouldn't have become a soldier in the army/military/navy or whatever Armed Forces unit you belong to. How does it feel to be separated from everyone and everything you know and love? I couldn't even handle being away at a Christian Camp for three days... a Christian Camp (just to let you know, it wasn't really a Christian camp, but rather a regular summer camp where you had church every day)!

In all actuality, I cant even imagine what I would be like being a soldier in the Armed Forces; I don't know if I'd be brave enough to enter the Armed Forces. It is because of my own insecurities that I look up to and admire the people who choose, out of free will, to fight for and serve their country; you are one of those people.

Keep going, be strong, and remember: Hope, confidence, and trust are everything!

All My American Love,

Lindsay

Green Bay, WI

Dear friend serving overseas,

I may not know your name but I am convinced that there are no coincidences. You were meant to receive this letter. We have an awesome God who cares about every event in our lives. I don't know what state of mind or what concerns you are presently facing but I want to be a voice that say's I care and that I am praying for you. Thank you so very much for being willing to leave your family, friends, and familiar surroundings to serve for this great country of ours. It is so true that freedom is not free. There is a price to pay and you are doing that for those you love as well as those that you don't even know. I don't know where your faith lies, but I am hoping that you have faith in Another One who also was willing to lay down His life for others, you and me both-Jesus Christ. There is a Bible verse, which says,

"No greater love has man than this, that he lay down his life for his friends."
John 15:13

Thank you for willingly giving of yourself in this time of war. I will be praying for your protection and that you will be delivered safely back to these shores. I am also praying that you and those you serve with will share some great memories, heartfelt humor and experiences that will have a positive impact in your life. Our experiences are never wasted.

I'd also like to let you know that there are many of us who grieve over the way the recent prison atrocities have prompted some, especially in the media to portray our military as untrained and inhumane. We know better. The awful actions of a few do not represent those, I know personally and like yourself who are serving with great training. conviction and courage. Please do not lose heart. We are not that gullible.

About myself, I'm a mom of 2 teenage boys, ages 13 and 16. One of them attends Lutheran High School where the "Million Letters of Thanks" project was started by a freshman student. My husband knows what it's like to be a part of the military as his father was a lieutenant colonel, in the Air Force as a test pilot. Their family moved all over the country from the east and finally ended up on the west coast at Edwards Air Force Base. He also made sacrifices for this country, was involved in several wars and even went to Vietnam when he was 40 years of age. I thank God for brave men and women like him and yourself. Thank You, Thank You, Thank You....

Well, it's time for me to take my boys to get their hair cut. The routine stuff of life...

Blessings,
Jeannie

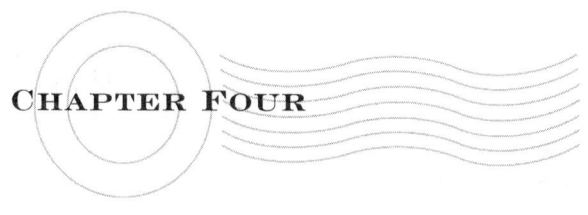

CHAPTER FOUR

Friends in the Fast Lane

I SUPPOSE EVERY TEENAGER—maybe it's every person, really—is at least a little fascinated by celebrities. They're famous, they live different lives from the rest of us, and they just seem very glamorous. When I started "A Million Thanks," I never expected that it would lead me to meet any celebrities, but I have in fact had a few brushes with fame.

I got to talk to Arnold Schwarzenegger on the phone while I was doing an interview with Roger Hedgecock, and he told me he thought I was doing a great job. That was incredibly cool. Senator Barbara Boxer wrote me a really nice letter, as did Reverend Robert Schuller, pastor of the Crystal Cathedral. The Crystal Cathedral is not too far from our house and we like to attend services there, as well as at our regular church, Light of the Canyon UMC in Anaheim. Pastor Rick Warren contacted me too, and he sent along auto-graphed copies of *The Purpose-Driven Life* and *The Purpose-Driven Life: Selected Thoughts and Scriptures for the Graduate*.

I was so surprised that these very successful people, who have very busy schedules, took the time to contact and thank me. I didn't feel I deserved these thank-yous, but those words sure felt good coming from them. To get an unso-licited thank-you is such a good feeling. It gave me some idea of the feeling our soldiers have when they get a "Million Thanks" letter.

I got to meet this year's *American Idol* finalists 3 through 10 (the top two were busy doing something else) at a NASCAR event. At the same event I met Gretchen Wilson, whose song "Redneck Woman" was #1 on the country music charts last year, and who'd won a Country Music Association Award and an American Music Award.

A really fun time was getting to meet Raven-Symone, Carly Patterson, Michael Phelps, Chad Michael Murray, and Amber Tamblyn when I received the Born to Lead Award from *Cosmo Girl* magazine.

Actor Gary Sinise e-mailed me early in my campaign and even offered to help us deliver letters overseas. He started an impressive program with author Laura Hillenbrand called Operation Iraqi Children, which gets Iraqi kids school supplies. It's nice to see a movie and TV star do more than just throw money at a charity. I really appreciated his willingness to help "A Million Thanks." When he put on his Web site a link to mine, it really helped to increase my site's traffic.

All of these encounters with famous people were exciting. My biggest "celebrity meeting," though, came in November. I'll tell you about that one later.

The celebrity I've spent the most time with is country music superstar John Michael Montgomery. It all started when Pastor Detviler asked me if I'd heard his song "Letters from Home." I hadn't, but as soon as I listened to it, I felt an immediate connection. It's about soldiers getting letters while they're away at war, and the video that goes with it just makes everyone cry. "Letters from Home" felt like the theme song for "A Million Thanks."

A short while after I first heard it, I did a radio interview with WIVK in Knoxville, Tennessee. The DJ doing the interview was named Gunner. I mentioned that I'd just heard this great song and would love to get in touch with the singer.

"You mean John Michael Montgomery?" he said. "I know John. Do you want me to get him on the phone right now?"

"Right now?" I said, a little surprised. "Uh, sure."

Sure enough, Gunner called John Michael's cell phone

and introduced me. John Michael was sitting in a doctor's office at the time. We talked for a while about "A Million Thanks" and about "Letters from Home." I told him I'd be happy to do anything I could to promote his song through my campaign, because I loved it so much and it had such a wonderful message. He said he thought what I was doing sounded really exciting and that we should try to hook up through his management people. The funny thing was that I thought we were off the air, but later I got e-mails from people saying they'd heard us on the radio together. I was just amazed that I got to talk to someone that big *at all*—I mean, most of my friends didn't know who he was, but he's sold something like twenty million CDs.

The next day, John Michael's record company called my dad and said they were extremely excited about the idea of getting John Michael together with me. They brainstormed for a while and put together a few tentative ideas. The day after that, I was called out of a class because my dad was on the phone.

"I've got some great news but you have to do this fast," he said. "You have to go to your phone (he was talking about the one at the desk the school had set up for me just outside the teachers' lounge) and call CMT (Country Music Television). They have John Michael Montgomery on live right now and they want you to surprise him." I ran down the hallway toward my "telephone desk."

The person who was interviewing John Michael on

CMT said, "I heard you've been talking to this girl who is doing something called 'A Million Thanks.'"

"Oh yeah," John Michael said. "I talked to her, and what she's doing is really great. She wants to use 'Letters from Home' in her campaign."

"Well, we have someone on the phone that would like to say hi to you."

John Michael was stunned when he heard it was me and I felt a little weird about surprising him like that, but we had a great conversation right on live national television. At the end, John Michael told everyone that we were going to be doing some things together to promote my campaign. As far as I knew, my dad and his managers were still trying to arrange something, but I guess John Michael just cut to the chase.

The first thing we did was a huge country music talk show called *After MidNite with Blair Garner*. That was the first time I got to meet John Michael in person and I liked him immediately. He seemed so nice and so real, unlike the way a lot of other celebrities appear. He said some great things about "A Million Thanks," and I realized that if I could get even a portion of his fans to write letters, we could make a lot of soldiers happy. Blair was also awesome, putting a link to my Web site on his, which has turned out to be one of my biggest referral sites.

Next, we went to Nashville together to do a two-day

radio tour of all the biggest country stations in America. We just sat in a studio while all of these stations did interviews with us, one after the other. Each station—more than seventy in all—got a six-minute window to do their interview. I heard that a number of stations were turned away. I'd like to think it was because they were all dying to get to talk to Shauna Fleming, but I knew who the real star was in this operation.

The radio tour was fantastic. We did five hours straight one day and seven hours straight the next. We even skipped lunch, which isn't the best thing for me, since I get kind of cranky when I don't eat. This was one of the best experiences of my life. In two days, we let a huge number of people know about "A Million Thanks" and I got to hang out with a country music superstar. I never was much of a country music fan—I really only listen to Christian music—but now, when we listen to country in the weight room while my basketball team works out, I have a whole new appreciation for it.

While I was on the Nashville trip, I got to meet Freddy Mullins, the actor who played the lead role in the great "Letters from Home" video. I'd wanted to meet him from the first time I saw the video, because he was so good in it. When it turned out that he lived in Nashville, we arranged to meet for dinner. He said he could only spend a half hour, but we stayed together for two and a half hours, talking about making videos, acting, and his experience with the actual soldiers in the video (only he and one other person were actors).

Freddy said he could relate to the soldiers. He felt he had some idea of what they were going through and the sacrifices they made, because one of his best friends had been killed in Iraq, and then later one of his wife's cousins was killed as well. He started to tear up just telling me about it. He said that it made the acting job he'd done on "Letters from Home" that much more meaningful for him. It hadn't taken anything for him to cry on the video because all he'd had to do was think about his friend.

During this time I did quite a bit of traveling, which I love to do. I made it a point to bring paper and pens with me on all my flights and to let the flight attendants know about my campaign. The flight attendants would make an announcement about it to the passengers and pass out paper for them to write thank-you letters. Most passengers did so enthusiastically. I remember one lady, though, who actually told the Southwest flight attendant that she didn't have time. I laughed when the attendant responded, "Well, you're not going to be going anywhere for three-and-a-half hours!"

A few weeks after our radio tour in Nashville, John Michael and I were together again at the Coca-Cola 600 in Charlotte. Before the race, John Michael sang "Letters from Home" to the more than two hundred thousand people in the stands and I stood onstage with him, handing out letters to soldiers. I tried not to think about the fact that there were a couple of hundred thousand people watching me, but the whole thing was pretty amazing. It was also great watching John Michael with the soldiers after the performance. He took a long time with every soldier he met, joking with them and thanking them for what they were doing. He really is a great guy.

The Coca-Cola 600 may have been my biggest experience with NASCAR, but it wasn't my only one. My first contact with a NASCAR team was at nearby Irwindale Speedway. Local Orange County drivers Kevin O'Connell and Scott Calvin heard about "A Million Thanks" and agreed to put the Web site address on the back quarter-panels of their cars to promote my campaign. Irwindale Speedway is a "short track," meaning a half mile around. It can hold only ten thousand fans (small by NASCAR standards), but it was still awesome to see WWW.AMILLIONTHANKS.ORG on the side of a car racing around the track.

Superstar NASCAR driver Matt Kenseth's wife is my kindergarten teacher's niece. When she told him about "A Million Thanks," he arranged for me to have a booth at a race next to the DeWalt booth (they're one of his biggest sponsors). That got the campaign a ton of attention. Meeting Matt Kenseth and his wife, Katie, was cool, too. Katie took the time to come over to our booth to write some letters to the soldiers. She signed them, "Love, Matt and Katie Kenseth." I could just imagine a soldier in Iraq who is a NASCAR fan getting that letter.

My favorite NASCAR people are the ones with the military cars. The cars have colorful designs and the name of a service branch in large letters across the hood. There is a car for almost every branch of the armed forces. Greg Biffle, who drives the National Guard car, is a great guy, and I really like everyone on the team. It probably has something to do with their being part of the military, but I just feel like they understand what I'm trying to do and go out of their way to help.

Overall, NASCAR has been fantastic. *NASCAR* and *NASCAR Scene* magazines have done articles about "A Million Thanks," and racetracks have made announcements about the campaign at every race where I've set up my letter collection booth. They say they'd like me to come to every race and I would love to do just that, but if I did, I'd never be in school because there's a NASCAR event just about every weekend. They're fun people to hang out with when I get the chance, though. I even got to go down to the pits one time at California Speedway. It was incredibly exciting, though it was also a little scary with tires and gas pumps and cars flying everywhere.

NASCAR is my favorite spectator sport. I was never really a fan until I got involved with "A Million Thanks," but I'm a big fan now. My Grandpa Richard has been a

NASCAR fan for more than fifty years, probably from the time NASCAR started. Every time we are with him on a Sunday, you can bet the TV is tuned to a race. It was really fun for me to meet some of his favorite drivers.

Some of my friends think it's weird that I like to watch cars go around in circles, but I think everything about the races is great. I love that they have a pastor or race chaplain go up and say a prayer at the beginning of each race. I don't know of any other sport that does that. And the fans are *so* patriotic. Our booths are always incredibly busy with fans who want to write letters. Getting involved with NASCAR has given a huge boost to the campaign.

★ ★ ★

OVERALL, encountering famous people has been fun. I'm always trying to meet up with more celebrities because I think that if they support the program, their fans will write letters. But to me, the biggest stars are the soldiers. There's nothing a singer, an actor, an athlete, a writer, or even a state governor could do to compare with what our soldiers do for us every day of the year.

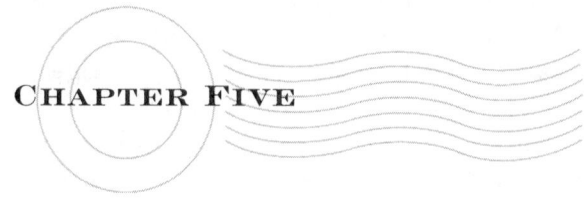

CHAPTER FIVE

The Millionth Letter

FOR MOST PEOPLE, lots of new things happen in the fall: school starts for kids, adults get back to work after summer vacations, the weather changes (although it doesn't change much here in Southern California), and you start thinking about Thanksgiving and Christmas. For "A Million Thanks," though, I knew that a different kind of new thing was going to happen: we were going to reach our goal. As the school year started, we exceeded 999,000 letters and e-mail messages received. I could hardly wait for the mail to come every day.

A few days into September, I found a big box sitting in the mailroom. It came from a high school in Missouri and contained a ton of letters. I knew for a fact that one of these letters would be number one million, and I found the thought electrifying. We hadn't set up any new sorting parties (and I couldn't wait for one anyway), so I took the box home with me after classes. The school that sent the letters packaged them in bundles, and my family and I patiently

sorted through them the way we had on countless occasions before. Then we got to it. Sitting on top of one of the bundles was our millionth letter. I pulled it out and took just a second to cherish the moment—I knew this was coming from the day I started "A Million Thanks"—then I read the message that Stephanie Cope, a junior at Francis Howell North High School in St. Charles, Missouri, had for our troops.

Thank you for all of
your hope and strength
in protecting our country.
Each day is one more
step toward a terror
free world. Again, thank
you for your service.
Hope you get home
soon!
♡ Stephanie
C.

It felt great to hold this letter in my hands. Here was the proof that all of the hard work of everyone involved in the campaign was worth it. A funny thing happened right then, though. I realized that I'd only achieved my *first* goal in this campaign, and that I had already established a new one before I even counted the millionth letter.

"I want to get one-point-four million letters," I said to my dad. He knew exactly why I'd come up with that number: there are one-point-four million active members of the American military. After seeing how much "A Million Thanks" had meant to me, he also knew why I would say something like that while I still had the millionth letter in my hands. He smiled and nodded, and we went through the rest of the box to begin the tally toward our new goal.

The next day, we called Francis Howell North High School to let them know that one of their students was our one millionth correspondent. Everyone there was *so* excited. The principal of the school, Dr. Darlene Jones, was ecstatic. She sounded like she'd won the lottery. The school had sent letters before—this latest box had come from their members of the National Honor Society—and they were thrilled to be such a big part of our campaign. They even invited me to come out to speak at the school.

I told my friends about reaching the one-million-letter goal and they were *so* happy. So many of them had played such a big part in making this a reality; I'm sure they took a lot of satisfaction in knowing we had made it. Everyone wanted us to have a big celebration right away, but I decided to hold off on it. Since the original plan was to tie "A Million Thanks" into National Military Appreciation Month, I decided we would have our celebration when the next one came around, in May 2005.

From the very beginning of the campaign, I knew what I wanted to do with the millionth letter: I wanted to present it to President Bush, our commander in chief. I realized this was thinking big, but as you may have guessed by now, I don't let big challenges intimidate me. I told my dad that this was my dream for the millionth letter and he set out to help me make it come true. We sent a couple of letters to the White House and then made contact with our local Congressmen, Ed Royce and Christopher Cox. Ed Royce, whom I met at one of the local "town hall" meetings he holds regularly, agreed to bring a letter from us directly to the President's secretary. This led to a series of phone conversations with the White House, and the President's scheduling office said there was a chance I might be able to meet the President.

If I did get to meet him I wanted to make a special presentation of the millionth letter, so we went to Fast Frame, a high-quality framer in Orange. We told the designer/manager what we needed and what we were going to do with the letter, and he took charge after that. He did an amazing job of framing the letter using red, white, and blue mattes. Then, to top it off, like so many other generous people I've encountered during this campaign, he refused any payment for his work. He'd done a gorgeous job worthy of hanging someday in the presidential library, and didn't take a penny for it.

We already had plans in place to go to New York in November for the Born to Lead Awards, and decided to make a trip to Washington part of our itinerary in case our chance to meet the President arose. The day before we were to leave for New York, I received the call we'd desperately hoped to receive. President Bush's office said I was being invited to visit him in the Oval Office. A whole set of emotions ran through me in a millisecond, from joy to excitement to a huge sense of accomplishment to an absolute fear that I would say something stupid to the President—or maybe not be able to speak at all—when I was with him.

In eighth grade, my class had gone to Washington. I'd been one of four students selected to lay a wreath at the Tomb of the Unknown Soldier at Arlington Cemetery. My dad arranged for our entire family to do it on this trip. I knew that this time, however, the ceremony would have an entirely different meaning for me. As we stood ready and listened to the instructions from the Tomb of the Unknowns Honor Guard, I began to think of what this ceremony was all about. We were laying a wreath of flowers, a ring of appreciation, in front of this large, beautiful white monument symbolizing the unidentified who'd lost their lives in past wars.

This was a special moment, a solemn moment. It was also a moment to realize how much my vision of the world had changed since I'd been in eighth grade.

As the meeting date with the President approached, my entire family was so excited. My older brother, Justin, who is a firefighter/paramedic, and his wife, Trisha, were able to fly out to be with us. Justin got permission from his captain to wear his fire department dress uniform. He looked great. Everyone did. Even my little brother looked impressive.

After checking in at the White House visitor office, we went to the Rose Garden where we assembled with other invited guests of the President's annual Thanksgiving turkey pardoning event. It was a perfect day with blue skies and a slight chill in the air. The White House provided hot cider and hot chocolate for us while we waited.

We were soon ushered to just outside of the Oval Office. Dozens of television cameras and photographers focused on the presidential podium. Each seat there had a name on it, and I was surprised to find that ours were in the front row. The turkey to be pardoned was named "Biscuits" and he waited patiently.

Soon President Bush appeared along with Vice President Cheney. The President made some humorous opening statements about the turkey and then granted him a presidential pardon. It was a warm, lighthearted moment.

After the ceremony, my family and I were taken into the White House to an area next to the Oval Office. We were all a bit nervous, wanting to make the most of our short time with the most powerful man in the world. I entered first, carrying the framed millionth letter. The President said, "Welcome everyone to the White House. Come on in." He was so friendly and his voice was calming. I was surprised that our meeting was so private. It was just my family, the President, his photographer, and his two young staff aides.

He asked me about "A Million Thanks." I answered him as quickly as I could, trying to get in as much detail as possible. I then said, "Mr. President, I would like to present you the one millionth thank-you letter collected for our troops." He took the frame from me, laid it on his desk, and read the inscription. He then told me how proud he was to have the letter given to him, and how much he appreciated what I was doing to support our troops.

I'm sure he was aware that we were in awe of standing with him in the Oval Office. He said, "You know, sometimes people come into the Oval Office and are so nervous they miss so much of the history that is here. Let me give you a tour." He proceeded to take us on this fabulous tour of his office, telling us why he had picked certain works of art and other items. He explained that the eagle on the Presidential Seal—carved in the front of his beautiful desk—held arrows, representing war, in one talon; and olive branches, representing peace, in the other. The eagle's head faced the arrows. He then pointed out the round carpet in his office designed by his wife, Laura. It had the same Presidential

Seal—except the eagle in the carpet faced the olive branches.

"You always have to make sure you have enough arrows to keep the peace," he said with a laugh.

Our meeting with the President lasted almost fifteen minutes and was another life-changing experience. I felt so humbled by the fact that the President had actually taken time out of his schedule to meet my family and me. As we left, all I could think of was, "Wow! I actually met the President of the United States!" It was the latest in a series of amazing experiences related to "A Million Thanks."

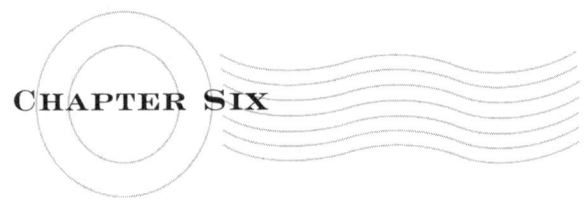

CHAPTER SIX

Feels Like a Million Miles

I'D BE LYING if I didn't say it felt great to reach my goal, and to reach heights that I know some people had thought were crazy to aim for. But I really feel like I'm at the beginning of this, rather than near the end. People tell me that, now that I've gotten a million letters, I need to close down the campaign and move on. I can't, though, and I know that I won't even when I get to my new goal of 1.4 million. This campaign has been my life. I have lots of other things going on—school, basketball, theater—but if I didn't have "A Million Thanks," I don't know what I'd do with myself. The people I've connected with during this campaign—especially the soldiers—are much too important to me, and I intend never to let them down.

In some ways, I can't remember what my life was like before "A Million Thanks." It was less than a year ago when I walked into my dad's office and told him I wanted to do something for the troops. In the months that have passed, though, it feels like I've traveled a million miles down a new path, and I have had a lifetime's worth of experiences. These experiences have enriched me in so many ways, making me humbler, wiser, and more aware of my fellow human beings than ever before. I've stood on stage in front of two hundred thousand people, appeared on national television, received a Born to Lead Award from *Cosmo Girl* magazine, been named one of the "Hottest 25" by *OC Metro* (along with, among others, baseball MVP Vladimir Guerrero and Mickey Mouse!), and sat in the Oval Office with President Bush. Yet I've come to realize that there's nothing I can ever accomplish to match what each and every American soldier does for our country.

Working on a campaign like "A Million Thanks" has been unbelievably rewarding and fulfilling, and I implore every young person out there to get involved in community service. It obviously doesn't have to be as big as the campaign I got involved in, but you'd be surprised at how a little project can turn into something very big if you really put your heart into it.

Here are some of the things I've learned about orchestrating a public service program that might be useful to anyone interested in starting one of their own:

Treat it like a mini-business. If you're going to get the most out of your public service program, you need to take it as seriously as a small businessperson takes his company. If the guy who runs the local card store decided to keep the store open ten hours one day, three hours the next, and maybe take a couple of days off after that, he wouldn't have the store for very long, would he? The same is true with your public service program. If you're going to get involved in one, you need to be dedicated to it, and that means putting in the hours every day.

If you take your project lightly, things will go downhill quickly—and once something begins to go badly, it takes so much more work to fix it than it would have taken to keep it running smoothly from the beginning. Think about what it's like in school. If you fall behind in your studies and start getting bad grades, it takes twice as much work to bring your grades up than it would have taken to get good grades from the beginning. Make sure to take care of the little things as soon as you get a chance, rather than putting them off for later. Little things tend to gather in big piles pretty quickly—and then all of a sudden you're stretched for time and forced to make compromises that you wouldn't need to make if you'd taken care of things as they came up.

Have a clear sense of your vision, but remember to be flexible. It's really important to set goals for yourself. What do you want to accomplish today? A month from now? Six months from now? What's your overall message? How are you getting that message across to the public? Make sure you understand these things, but at the same time, don't be so rigid that you can't try out different things or leave a little room for improvisation. So many opportunities came to me because I didn't follow my agenda completely. Even deciding to stop at Starbucks before going to a meeting led me to meet people who contributed important things to "A Million Thanks"—I simply wouldn't have met these people if I hadn't made this unscheduled pit stop.

Things are going to come up; you have to expect the unexpected, whether it's something great or something that seems to mess things up for you. Make sure that you have an outline for your program and an agenda for the coming days, but definitely expect to plan as you go. Otherwise, you might miss a little sidetrack that will lead you somewhere great.

Prioritize, prioritize, prioritize. Let me say that one more time: *prioritize.* Ask yourself this question about every single task associated with your program: Is this going to help me take this campaign further? If the answer is yes, then get to it. If the answer is no, then forget about it, at least for now. The same is true with everything else that happens in your life while you're working on your campaign. Which things are most important to you? Which can you do without, even if you don't *really* want to do without them? You're going to need to sacrifice one thing for another at different times during your campaign. Get used to making these choices.

At the same time, don't sell yourself short. You might be surprised by how much you can handle. Test your limits. If you have two big things going on in your life—school and your public service program, for instance—does that mean you can't play a sport or work on the yearbook staff as well? Check it out. Try that third big thing. If it turns out to be too much, scale back. You might find, though, that if it means enough to you, you can handle it. Push yourself to get outside your box. Sometimes when things seem really tough, if you push a little harder, you'll realize you can do so much more.

Accept roadblocks and failures. I guarantee that your campaign is not going to go smoothly 100 percent of the time. You're going to run into problems, something is not going to be available when you need it, and you're going to have a bad day and screw something up. Don't get flustered and don't panic.

I recently saw two great posters that really inspired me. One was for the Marine Corps and it read, "Pain is weakness leaving the body." The other showed pictures of four people and a list of their significant failures. These guys really bombed out. Yet all four of them learned from their mistakes—and became United States presidents. The headline on that poster read, "If at first you don't succeed, you're in good company." The point here is that you can't consider yourself a failure if something goes wrong, because even wildly successful people fail. And the pain associated with this will not only go away in time, but will leave you stronger. Find something good in every failure. The worst thing you can possibly do is sit and cry in your room.

You can't get other people to join you unless what you are doing comes from your heart. A public service program is all about helping others, not about personal glory. Don't start on a program like this unless the campaign really, really matters to you. If your heart isn't in it, people will see right through you and they won't want to contribute to your efforts. This is a real problem because you can't do anything big without the help of a lot of people. On the other hand, if you care deeply about the issue of your campaign, people will get caught up in your passion and jump at the opportunity to help you out any way they can—just look at how many people gave their time, their energy, and their money to "A Million Thanks."

Get the word-of-mouth going. The best way to get attention for your public service program is to get people within your community talking about it. Tell your friends, your siblings, and your teachers about it. If you get them excited, they'll tell *their* friends, siblings, and other teachers. Then those people will tell other people and soon a lot of people will know about it and the project will begin to come to life.

In getting attention via word-of-mouth, it's important to keep your message simple and avoid getting off track. Do you remember the game "Telephone," where a line of people whisper something from one person to the next and, by the time you get to the end of the line, what the last person heard is completely different from what the first person said? Word-of-mouth works the same way if your message is too complicated. Keep it really clear—mine was, "I'm collecting thank-you letters for the troops"—there will always be time to expand on your message once a large base of people know about it.

If you can get any media attention, go for it. You might be a little camera shy or scared to death of public speaking, but if you can get the media to pick up on your project, it will be a huge help. You don't need to shoot for the *Today* show or *DaySide with Linda Vester* right away. Most local radio and TV stations like to do pieces about kids doing cool things, and if one station covers you, there's a really good chance that this will lead to another media opportunity. This kind of thing tends to spread outward—suddenly you might start getting calls for interviews from halfway across the country.

When appearing in the media, try to know who you're talking to and anticipate any questions they might ask to get you off track. I learned this the hard way. It's not necessarily that reporters want to undermine your message or get you to say something you don't mean, but their agenda isn't the same as yours. If you know that a particular radio station tends to cover stories in a particular way or tries to catch their interview subjects off guard, you'll be prepared when they try this on you, and you'll be ready to stick to your message. When faced with a question I don't want to answer, one of my favorite tricks—I learned this from watching politicians and celebrities on television—is to answer a question I *do* want to answer instead. Reporters probably won't challenge you, and if viewers and listeners are interested in what you're saying, they won't even notice that you didn't answer the question asked.

News or press releases about what you are doing get your message into the hands of the media. There is a specific format to follow; if you don't, your release will be ignored, as media editors receive countless releases each day. Remember, too, that your release must be interesting and have an eye-catching title. There are many sites on the Internet that can give you all the information you need to write a good news release. You can distribute your release via fax or e-mail to most newspaper, radio, and television outlets. Their contact information is usually included on their Web site.

"A MILLION THANKS" continues to be an amazing experience for me. As I said earlier, I have no intention of stopping the campaign anytime soon. My ultimate goal is to let every American service member and veteran know that their country appreciates them and honors their sacrifice. I have to admit that when I started "A Million Thanks," I didn't really know what our soldiers went through on a daily basis. Now that I have a better idea, I appreciate them so much more. I'm in awe of what they face, especially when I compare it to my easy life. I could never do what they do, putting their lives in danger all the time. Roller coasters are about as much excitement as I can handle. That these people face real peril not once, but repeatedly, and that they're currently doing it in a war where you can't even be certain who the enemy is, is incredibly humbling to me.

At the same time, I know that what we're doing for them with "A Million Thanks" helps. When you're putting yourself in harm's way for your country, it means something to know that what you're doing matters to the people at home. From the conversations I've had with service members and their families, I know "A Million Thanks" has made a difference in their lives.

I guess my final—and biggest—message in this book is that I'm living proof that one person can make a difference. I had tons and tons of help with "A Million Thanks," but it started with a single idea. What's *your* big idea that can make a huge difference in one person's life or in the lives of many? There are so many things each and every one of us can do to improve the world a little bit at a time. You just need to decide you're going to do it.

Somebody sent me a great story from the Internet recently. It was about a nerdy kid, a total loner who others picked on all the time. One day, the kid was walking down the hall when one of the school jocks knocked his books out of his hands. A third kid, rather than just passing by or laughing at him, helped him pick up his books and talked to him for a while. They started hanging out together and became really good friends, even though one was a loner and the other traveled with the popular crowd. A couple of years later, the loner was so inspired by this act of friendship that he wound up valedictorian of the school. In his commencement speech, he told his fellow students something he'd never told anyone before—that the day the books were knocked out of his hands, he had become so frustrated with life that he was planning to kill himself that night. The kid who helped him pick up his books literally saved his life.

I'm a firm believer in the power of one. We all have the ability to leave a positive mark on the world. And for those of you who choose to do so, let me say from my heart:

"A Million Thanks!"